DRUMS ALONG THE CONGO ◆

Books by Rory Nugent

The Search for the Pink-Headed Duck

Drums Along the Congo

RORY NUGENT ◆ DRUMS
ALONG
THE
CONGO

▲◆▼▲◆▼▲◆▼▲◆▼▲◆▼▲◆▼▲◆▼▲◆▼▲◆▼▲◆▼▲◆▼▲◆▼

On the Trail of Mokele-Mbembe,
the Last Living Dinosaur

HOUGHTON MIFFLIN COMPANY
BOSTON   NEW YORK   1993

For information about permission to reproduce selections from this book,
write to Permissions, Houghton Mifflin Company, 215 Park Avenue South,
New York, New York 10003.

Library of Congress Cataloging-in-Publication Data
Nugent, Rory.
    Drums along the Congo : on the trail of Mokele-Mbembe, the last
living dinosaur / Rory Nugent.
    p.   cm.
    ISBN 0-395-58707-7 (cloth)   ISBN 0-395-67071-3 (pbk.)
    1. Mokele-mbembe.   2. Congo River — Description and travel.
3. Zaire — Description and travel — 1981–   4. Nugent, Rory —
Journeys — Congo River.   5. Nugent, Rory — Journeys — Zaire.
I. Title.
    QL89.2.M58N84   1993
    916.751 — dc20   92-47251
                    CIP

Printed in the United States of America

DOH 10 9 8 7 6 5 4 3 2 1

Again, James Angell

Listen to the creepy proclamation,
Blown through the lairs of the forest-nation,
Blown past the white-ants' hill of clay,
Blown past the marsh where the butterflies play: —
"Be careful what you do,
Or Mumbo-Jumbo, God of the Congo,
And all of the other
Gods of the Congo,
Mumbo-Jumbo will hoo-doo you,
Mumbo-Jumbo will hoo-doo you,
Mumbo-Jumbo will hoo-doo you."

— Vachel Lindsay, *The Congo*

CHAPTER ◆ I

THE WITCH DOCTOR CURSES. No one told him it was an American coming for the cure. His black eyes bore into mine, probing for something deep inside me. Bright-colored plastic toothpicks pierce his earlobes, and a string of wooden fetishes bounce menacingly across his chest.

"Can you help?" Ambroise, my guide, challenges.

The witch doctor, Fortunado, winces and moves to the left, until our shadows no longer cross. He mumbles something inaudible and shakes his head.

"He has brought money," Ambroise offers as I pull out a wad of West African francs.

The witch doctor surveys me again. After a moment he announces that I'm dirty and that my stink offends the gods, but if I'm willing to pay the price, he will cleanse me of evil. As I hold out the cash, he's careful not to touch my hand. He nods after counting the bills.

"Déshabillez!" the witch doctor barks.

Off come my shoes and socks, but not fast enough.

"Vite! Vite!" He doesn't have all day. People all over the Congo await him. He has potions to concoct and spells to cast.

Grabbing the front of my shirt, he repeats in French, "To skin . . . to skin." For good measure, he kicks my shoes across the courtyard.

"Hurry, you're pissing him off," Ambroise hisses.

I've been in Brazzaville for over a month now, and I'm beginning to wonder if I'll ever be allowed beyond its limits. Congolese officials have been generous with their coffee and croissants, but not with their travel permits. My proposed destination, Lake Télé, fabled home of the supreme jungle deity, Mokele-Mbembe, is off-limits to foreigners without a special pass.

"Wear yourself naked," The witch doctor insists and gestures feverishly at my underwear. Reluctant, I thumb the elastic waistband, recalling how I arrived at this odd situation.

Yesterday, after a particularly long and unproductive meeting with government officials, Ambroise concluded that my approach was all wrong. I must first beseech Mokele-Mbembe and then petition the government for permission to visit Lake Télé.

"God before man," Ambroise insisted. "And to reach Mokele-Mbembe you must be cleansed . . . It's the only way."

A small group of men has gathered in the courtyard. The witch doctor scowls as Ambroise urges, "Do it . . . Come on, do it."

I suppose a few minutes of public nudity here in the dust of the Bacongo district, miles from my hotel, won't damage my reputation any further.

"Now we will begin." The witch doctor hurls my boxer shorts into the air.

He signals to Ambroise, and the two of them vanish into

the witch doctor's house, leaving me stark naked to the gawking crowd. A *mundélé*, or white man, let alone his genitals, is a rare sight in this neighborhood, and more and more men trickle into the courtyard fenced by a hodgepodge of mud bricks and stones.

I seek the shade and lean against a wall, trying to ignore the wide eyes staring at me. A mongrel trots over for a quick sniff and attempts to mount my leg. A kind gentleman calls the dog and boots it into the street.

Voices are coming from inside the house, but the words are muffled by drawn curtains imprinted with portraits of President Denis Sassou-Nguesso, the Maoist who rose to power in 1979. The talking continues, seconds tick by like hours, and my patience expires. I poke my head through the doorway, interrupting the clink of glasses. Ambroise and Fortunado are sitting comfortably at a table sipping whiskey.

"A toast to a successful cleansing." Ambroise hoists his glass.

"Oui." The witch doctor tosses back his drink and quickly refills his tumbler.

I turn on my heels with a loud harumph and storm back to the courtyard. The curious onlookers retreat to a safe distance as one agitated stranger scrambles for his clothes. The witch doctor bursts from the house and snatches the shirt from my hand. He waves a Fanta bottle filled with a thick, golden liquid.

"Regardez!" He jiggles the bottle.

Intrigued, I watch as he holds it up to the sun. Scores of insects are suspended in the amber goo, and he seems to be clicking his tongue at each one. He plucks a toothpick from his earlobe and jabs it into the neck of the bottle. Then a curious silence ensues. I wonder if the insects convey some cosmic meaning, a horoscope perhaps.

"Are the signs good?" I ask, eager to learn my lot.

"Silence!"

I have had Hindus predict the future from my shadow, and Tibetan lamas have divined my fate from blades of grass tossed in the air, but this oracle of insects is new to me. Most soothsayers in this area rely on a divining board sprinkled with sand; the believer shakes the board, and the resulting lines are interpreted by an Ife-trained fortuneteller. I look for Ambroise, who is moving through the crowd, proudly telling people that he's the one who has brought the mundélé.

"Ambroise! What does the witch doctor see?"

Ambroise questions the priest in Lingala, an ancient Bantu language that has a soft, musical quality, with repetitive vowel sounds and drawn-out *f*'s.

"He sees many colors."

"What?"

He shrugs. "That's what he said . . . many pretty colors."

At last the witch doctor puts down the Fanta bottle and surrounds it with small rocks and dirt. He returns the toothpick to his left ear and removes his rings and bracelets. He motions me into the middle of the courtyard, exposing me to an unblinking equatorial sun. Almost immediately sweat begins to flow down my body, and I wonder how long it will be until my pink skin scalds. The sun's withering stare, Ambroise says, is essential to the cleansing process.

The witch doctor rises on the balls of his feet, stretches his arms skyward, and begins opening and closing his hands rhythmically. His eyes shut tight, he gulps mouthfuls of air to capture energy from the sky gods. Invigorated, he stomps toward me and exhales an unearthly, high-pitched scream.

"Ambroise," I plead from a puddle of sweat.

"Hush!"

The witch doctor spins like a dervish, whooping as he revolves. His necklace of fetishes dances to life, eerily animate. He raises one hand, bows, and, without warning, thrusts his contorted face into mine. Spittle sprays across my brow as he howls a painful sound. The crowd gasps in admiration. The witch doctor then tugs on his necklace and issues a spine-tingling trill for each fetish; I wonder if these vocal gymnastics are for the audience or the gods.

Suddenly the witch doctor becomes somber and assumes a look of intense concentration. He appears to fall into a trance: his eyes glaze, saliva foams in the corners of his mouth, liquid runs from his nose, and his limbs twitch spasmodically.

"It's working," Ambroise whispers. The people around him nod.

The sun is blazing hotter than ever, sapping my resolve. I can feel my bald pate frying, and a powerful thirst has seized me.

"Give me my hat."

"No! . . . You must be naked."

"I don't care. My hat, please!"

"Shhhh."

The witch doctor, disturbed by our voices, emerges from his trance and wags a finger. Everything is going well; impatience, however, will sabotage the cleansing. He says he was communing with the gods and has their ear. Ambroise suggests I think about ice cubes.

A young boy fetches a galvanized bucket from the side of the house. A red liquid sloshes over the rim. The witch doctor mutters an incantation while dipping his fingertips into the bucket. He flicks the liquid at me, splattering my body with crimson dots.

"Doorways for the evil spirits," Ambroise advises.

"Protect yourselves," someone in the crowd warns. Instantly the onlookers start praying, aware that the ousted devils will soon be seeking new homes.

The witch doctor steps back to examine his work and adds a few more dots around my feet and navel. Apparently satisfied, he invokes a new sequence of chants, this time kissing a fetish at the start of each one. I feel myself growing faint as the sweat continues to roll off me. My head and shoulders are the color of boiled lobsters. I groan when Fortunado instructs me to flap my arms like a bird.

"Inhale . . . exhale . . . inhale . . ." he orders.

"Drink the air he has purified. Force the devils out!" Ambroise coaches.

The witch doctor bows toward the sun and claps his hands twice. The crowd cheers as he turns and slaps the tender skin on my back.

"Success!" Ambroise trumpets. "You are clean . . . no more devils."

I thank the witch doctor and scurry for the shade. He chases after me and yanks me back into the sunlight. The ceremony is not over.

"Hold on. He must seal you from the new devils trying to get back in."

"What?"

"Silence!" The witch doctor picks up the solar-heated Fanta bottle and positions it directly over my head. With a blurp, the sacred potion plops onto my head, much to the amusement of the crowd. Slowly he spreads the jellied substance over my entire body, methodically working his way down to my toes.

The potion has a noxious odor that stings my nostrils. The stench alone should keep devils away. The crowd swings upwind, pinching their noses and dousing their handkerchiefs with perfume.

"I can hardly breathe!" I gag and shut my eyes, irritated by the goo.

"The potion is very powerful," Ambroise observes.

"What's in it?" A bittersweet taste creeps into my mouth. I can hear Ambroise talking to Fortunado as the liquid oozes between my buttocks.

"He says there are many ingredients. Some are secrets, but he did say crocodile oil and honey and bits of . . ."

I feel a tickling all over and, opening my eyes, I see that I'm shrouded with insects; flies dine on my torso; honeybees graze on my shoulders; tiny beetles crawl in my pubic hair; millipedes picnic in the shade of my insteps; a queue of black ants is working its way up my right leg. As I move to brush them off, the witch doctor pins my arms.

"Be strong," he says, his hands circling my wrists.

"Stand still," Ambroise adds, "and show the devils how strong you are."

The itching is unbearable. Every winged insect within a half kilometer has picked up the scent and swarmed to this six-foot-two-inch lollipop. I recall reading that the Bateke tribes upriver used a similar method to punish infidelity. An adulterer would be slathered with honey, bound to a tree deep in the rain forest, and left to be eaten piecemeal; supposedly the practice stopped decades ago.

"You should see yourself, très formidable," Ambroise pipes gleefully.

Cloaked with insects, I shimmer in the sunlight, a mosaic of iridescent wings, amethyst bodies, emerald fur, cobalt shells, yellow shields, and glistening eyes. The odor of the rancid potion knots my stomach. In the dust I spot a column of driver ants wending its way toward me; wasps start nibbling in the right crease of my crotch, arching their backs and exposing their stingers in a harvest dance.

"Please, O Holy One," I whine.

He finally releases his grip, saying that it's important for all the insects to return to the gods fat and happy. "You are free of devils . . . Now go to the river and wash."

"Follow him." Ambroise points to a boy running out of the courtyard.

Snatching up my cap and underwear, I streak off, shedding

bugs with every step. The young boy leads me down an un-
paved street that dead-ends at the Congo River. He jumps from
boulder to boulder and finally points out a rock pool close to
the river's edge. He hands me a bar of soap and takes a seat.
The crowd from the cleansing has followed and applauds the
witch doctor as he arrives. Fishermen leave their traps to see
what the commotion is all about. The goo does not scrub off
easily; I have to scour my already raw skin with mud and sand
before the soap does any good. Ambroise stands on the riverbank telling anyone who will listen that he's my redeemer.

"It took weeks to convince the mundélé . . . My prayers
worked . . . Yes, I arranged everything."

As I head to the main stream to rinse off, the boy jumps up
and grabs my arm. The deep water isn't safe, he signals. He
points beyond the fishing traps to a line of turbulence that
marks the beginning of the rapids and tosses a stick into the
river. We watch it spin convulsively downstream, caught in a
deceptively swift current. I submerge in the shallows.

"I hope you see Mokele-Mbembe," the witch doctor shouts
from the bank, turning to leave.

"Here are your clothes. I'll be at Fortunado's when you
finish." Ambroise jogs to catch up with the priest. They walk
arm in arm down the street and out of sight, followed by the
crowd and the young boy. The fishermen finish their cigarettes and go back to work.

Alone, I float on my back and close my eyes. An image of
the god-beast Mokele-Mbembe gradually comes to me. The
long, thin-necked sauropod is holding court on the lush shores
of Lake Télé. All sorts of jungle creatures are in attendance:
duikers, bongos, reedbucks, sitangs, okapis, jungle cats, galagos, chimps, and gorillas pay homage. Monkeys adorn the god
with liana necklaces strung with orchids and periwinkle; ori-
oles, sunbirds, hawk eagles, coucals, swifts, trogons, and parrots deposit fruit at its feet. The god-beast looks at me and

nods its gigantic head, as if to say, "Sure, come visit . . . we'll be expecting you."

◆

The next morning Ambroise and I meet outside his office building, a four-story cement blockhouse designed by Romanians, engineered by Chinese, and paid for by Soviets.

"You must be feeling great," Ambroise gushes as we stride toward the Ministry of Forests. "And you look so clean . . . Now you will surely get the permit."

However, I'm not issued a permit that day or even that month; in fact, my situation begins to deteriorate. The officials start asking me to pay for the coffee and croissants.

"Hmmm. Some devils must have returned. We should visit Fortunado again," Ambroise suggests, but I keep walking in the shade.

CHAPTER ◆ 2

A MBROISE AND I have been together for weeks now, and after a rocky start, we've formed a guarded friendship. He's a junior officer at the Ministry of Rural Development, where he specializes in writing grant proposals. Most health and sanitation projects needing foreign aid are routed across his desk. He claims to be good at his job, and I've come to believe him: he certainly knows how to weasel money out of me.

Ambroise was detailed to shadow my movements eighteen hours after I was arrested and charged with a possibly hostile act. It was a perfect day for birding, and I was strolling along the docks of Pointe Hollandaise, near the tip of Brazzaville's Plaine district. Since it was Sunday, cranes and forklifts were idle, and there were no workers about. I raised my binoculars to study a pair of fairy blue flycatchers, a rare sight this far from the forest. As I happily watched the acrobatic duo, their powder-blue bodies flashing in the sunlight, a hand came down hard on my shoulder. Three soldiers trained their rifles on me as I was frisked and led to jail. I spent the remainder of the day convincing the commandant of police that I was not a capitalist spy scrutinizing harbor installations. They finger-printed me, filed reports, and stripped my cameras of film.

An unsuspecting Ambroise on his day off, loafing in a comrade's office far from the docks, answered the phone.

"I told the major I wasn't the person he wanted," Ambroise recounted later, "but he didn't care. He demanded my name, office, and section number, and hung up. New orders were on my desk the next morning."

When we were introduced, Ambroise handed me a document identifying him as my "official escort," an assignment he clearly regarded with contempt. We exchanged all of two dozen words our first day together and not many more during the ensuing week but, stuck with each other, we have been forced to work things out.

Ambroise and I spend our days in government offices, inching up the bureaucratic ladder, meeting civility with untiring civility. In the evenings he shepherds me around Brazzaville to his favorite nightclubs, for music, especially the sort pulsing from the bars frequented by Cuban soldiers, is his passion. Many of the soldiers are on leave from neighboring Angola, where a civil war still rages, fueled by money and munitions from Russia and America. The Cubans have been a presence here since the mid-sixties, and Fidel's troops brought their horns as well as their rifles. They've successfully rewoven the Latin rhythms to the older African beats. The result, as one sergeant tells me, "shakes your treetops."

Ambroise and I hook up after dinner near his home just off Independence Avenue, a kilometer-long strip of government housing, small markets, fruit stands, and social clubs. On my first visit to his local boîte, the Palm Club, the other patrons filed out, scowling and muttering unpleasantries about mundélés as they passed. Now my presence is tolerated, and sometimes a barfly will even ask me an innocuous question — invariably something to do with American pop culture. The Congolese are big fans of Hollywood, rock-and-roll, and prime-time television.

▼

Tonight I have promising news to share with Ambroise. The deputy minister I've been trying to meet for weeks called my hotel and left a message. He wants to see me at nine o'clock tomorrow morning. Eager to tell Ambroise, I arrive a bit early at the Palm Club. The bartender, who is also the owner, digs deep into the plaid cooler and pulls out an icy Primus beer. He makes change from his pocket, with the large bills disappearing into his left boot. His name is Reuben: it says so eight times on his belt. "A souvenir," he told me, "from my first trip to Paris. I couldn't make money playing the drums there, and I didn't want to sell umbrellas, so I came back and started this place."

As usual the boom box, ensconced high on a shelf beyond the reach of meddling fingers, is blasting a conga. Live music will start later, depending on which bus the musicians are able to catch. Reuben jumps up on a chair and slips on a Tito Puente tape.

"He's almost an American," Reuben observes, tossing me the empty cassette box. Like most tapes sold in West Africa, it's a black-market product from Lagos, Nigeria.

I have my pick of tables; most of Reuben's patrons stand at the bar made from two-by-fours or lean against the white-washed walls, swaying to the music. Ambroise saunters in after a while, and I announce my news. He immediately demands a celebration, positive that my travel permit has been signed.

"He wouldn't meet with you to say no, that's what assistants are for . . . Big shots think of themselves as nice guys who get things done."

His optimism is contagious, and we start toasting our imminent departure in search of Mokele-Mbembe. Congo dinosaur. Jungle god-beast. Supreme forest deity. Here we come! After our fourth drink, Ambroise informs me that his per diem doubles if he leaves Brazzaville.

"What's wrong?" he asks, noting the furrows on my brow. For his work as my official escort, I already pay him a hefty salary established by the state.

"Encore, s'il vous plaît," I tell Reuben after tallying the cost of six weeks in the jungle with Ambroise.

For the first time, Ambroise pays for the drinks. "Cheer up," he consoles. "You will see Lake Télé, I will buy a new refrigerator."

Mildly soused, we decide to head over to the February Fifth Club, a hot spot with the best music in town. The date marks the inauguration of the present regime, when Colonel Sassou-Nguesso exchanged his jungle fatigues for the tailored suits befitting a president. Uncharacteristically, I decide to splurge on a cab, and as we climb into the battered Renault, the Palm Club empties. Everyone, including Reuben, has decided to join us. The cab driver choreographs the seating, while Reuben closes up the bar and leaves a note for the musicians. Eight of us manage to squeeze inside the cab, and four others cram into the open trunk. Riding dangerously low to the ground, we slowly wend our way along the dark streets, zigzagging around potholes.

"Do you know Lucy?" Reuben asks as the cab veers, missing a bicyclist by inches.

"Who?"

"Lucy — you know, Lucy on Kinshasa TV."

"Ah, that Lucy . . . sure." I watched an episode on the television in the hotel lobby.

"The band playing tonight at the club is very good, like Desi's, only better."

"Uh-huh," I say, watching the sparks fly as we bounce across a rut.

"Do you remember when Fred and Ethel . . . ?" Reuben and the cabbie are soon arguing about which episode is the funniest.

I tune them out and try to make some sense of our route. It's impossible, however, and I give up after the moon crosses the windshield for the fifth time. There are no street lights, and the driver seems phobic about paved roads.

We make our fourth U-turn. "Does anyone know where we are going?" I ask.

"No problem," Ambroise answers blithely. "We'll get there. Everybody makes wrong turns around here."

Brazzaville is a city without street signs. The mail is delivered to post office boxes, and only a few long-time civil servants in the Water Department know the official name of each byway. People living along small dead-end alleys often give the name of the nearest boulevard when asked their street address. The secret to navigating the city is to memorize landmarks, but at night without street lights, they are hard to spot.

We eventually arrive at the February Fifth Club to find dozens of cars and bicycles already parked in front. A giant neon palm tree with pulsing leaves is potted above the arched gateway. Glowing cigarette lighters reveal clusters of people in the shadows of a high wall enclosing the club grounds.

"It used to belong to a foreign government, I think, or maybe it was a mansion," Ambroise remarks, trying to explain the broken glass and barbed wire topping the wall.

"Back in sixty-three, we had all the French scared and sent the richest ones packing," Reuben says, referring to the Communist Party demonstrations that rocked the country and toppled the moderate government of Fulbert Youlou, a defrocked priest who rose to power with the blessings of the French. Reuben employed his skills as a bartender in the name of the revolution, claiming that nobody made a better Molotov cocktail than he.

"A shot of vermouth was the trick . . . Add that to gasoline and you have a knockout mix."

Two turbanned women on a moped wave at us as they zip in front of the cab's headlights. Their wave arouses the cabbie, who decides to join us for the evening. Once we disentangle our legs and get out of the cab, I hear a deep rumbling sound reminiscent of artillery fire in an old film.

"The rapids?"

"Oui, les rapides," four men chorus.

The sound of the water stirs me. As the others move toward the club, I stand alone, listening to the tumult.

The Fangs, a large tribe living downriver and along the coast, believe the gods all have individual voices. The sky gods have the snap of lightning and the boom of thunder; the earth gods issue tremors and groans; the wind gods whisper and howl; the fire gods crackle and snap; the various river gods rumble, sing, and sometimes purl.

What voice, I wonder, does Mokele-Mbembe have? A few Ubangi tribes say the god-beast hisses like a dragon; the Sanghas say it roars; others insist the deity murmurs like a slow-moving stream. Perhaps the river gods will tell me.

"Hey." Ambroise wraps an arm around my shoulder. "Les femmes are this way. Venez."

"I want to look at the river first."

Ambroise groans. "The river will always be there, the girls are only here tonight." I tell Ambroise to go ahead; I'll catch up with him and the girls later.

"Okay, but don't get into trouble," he says.

The moon is nearly full, rising above the twin stars in

Gemini. Slender black clouds jet inland on the prevailing southwesterly breeze. A stand of sugar palms bends to the wind, their leaves pointing upriver to the heart of the continent. Several feet away a candle bush droops into the path, its clusters of bright yellow flowers flickering.

As I approach the river, I can feel the earth shudder, a warning from the river gods perhaps. Clouds suddenly blanket the moon, and in the darkness I nearly trip over something; it's a bowl of fruit, most likely left by some earlier visitor seeking favor. I rearrange the fruit and add a chocolate bar of my own. The clouds come and go, and I slow my pace as a heavy mist envelops me. Ahead in the fickle light the pale Congo River emerges. The air is vaporous — each breath leaves droplets in my nostrils; there's no doubt that I've crossed into the domain of the river god. The sounds of rushing waves swirl into my head. All solid matter seems to have been distilled, rendered liquid, even the ground squishes underfoot. Pulling me to its edge is the resonating basso profundo of the Congo, moaning, dipping, and plunging. Preternatural ribbons of spume rise out of the water to greet me.

I grope in the darkness for a perch atop a boulder. A shaft of moonlight pierces the clouds and reveals a tableau vivant: the river's surface is a giant stage, its players diaphanous forms locked in a whirling dance. The moon blinks, but the riotous sounds echo the vanished image. The moonlight freezes a curtain of pearl droplets in space, then lingers on this vignette of ghostly water beings spinning skyward, corkscrewing up to the stars.

For centuries these rapids protected the African interior from inquisitive Westerners. Phoenicians were the first to sight the river, according to Herodotus, who told their story and dated their journey to the time of Pharaoh Necho (circa 600 B.C.). Later Xerxes was said to have sent ships around the Cape of Good Hope, but evidence is lacking; indeed, it's doubtful that any European investigated the river until 1482, when Diogo Cāo and his Portuguese crew sailed a caravel to the first cataract, nearly fifty miles from the ocean. The granite marker he erected there, claiming the river in the name of Lisbon's King John II, is still on the left bank. Subsequent Portuguese expeditions rarely ventured upstream more than a few miles. It was thought that only disease and death awaited the white man who went beyond the reach of the ocean breezes. Besides, the early settlers had come for slaves, and there were plenty to be bought along the coast from warring tribes eager to sell their prisoners. It has been estimated that seventeen million Africans were boarded on boats bound for the slave markets.

The British were next on the scene, but Her Majesty's government waited more than three centuries before charging James Kingston Tuckey with exploring the river. At the time (1816), royal geographers were positive that the Congo River was an inconsequential stream, but they hoped it would lead Tuckey to the Niger River. Though well financed and equipped, the expedition seemed jinxed from the start. Storms dogged them across the Atlantic, and three men were lost at sea; eighteen more died later, including the Irish-born Tuckey, after the ship anchored below the rapids.

Finally, in the 1870s Savorgnan de Brazza and Henry Stanley, leading separate expeditions, cracked open the dark interior and explored the river above the rapids, initiating the world's most obdurate land grab. De Brazza pushed south toward the river from Gabon and laid claim to a huge region, several times the size of France, which was later incorporated into French Equatorial Africa. Stanley rode the Congo from its headwaters, and his patron, King Leopold of Belgium, sought title to all the interior territory bounded by the left bank.

Thoughts of the past vanish as a spray of water drenches my clothing. Below me the river churns as waves crest, curl, and atomize, rudely slapping against ancient rocks, barreling forward in ceaseless turmoil. Off to my left, about ten yards away, columns of water shoot up the sides of two boulders. A tree trunk crashes by, tumbling end over end, a toothpick in the mouth of the god. I watch it plunge and then vault into the air, spat into the night. No doubt it will wedge somewhere else and be smashed to bits before reaching the Atlantic two hundred miles away. Its volume exceeding two Mississippis, the Congo seethes and rasps as it funnels into the narrow cataract below me.

A daredevil French team tried to shoot these rapids several months ago. A confident bunch with sophisticated equipment, they brazenly forwarded a celebratory case of champagne by land to the Cauldron of Hell, the last of the Congo's thirty-two cataracts. However, a few hours after embarking, the first boat capsized, and not long afterward the other craft also flipped. Several bodies were found near this spot, but the other crewmen disappeared. Similar fates have been dealt to hydroelectric surveyors attempting to tame the rapids, which, it has been estimated, could generate power for one third of the world's electrical needs.

I'm in no hurry to join Ambroise back at the club. The sound of the river is soothing, and the spray is a tangible realization of my adolescent dreams. When I unpacked bananas in a supermarket, I imagined myself cutting them down deep in the rain forest and loading the fruit on a steamer; pumping gas in the Berkshire Hills, I invented grand expeditions up this river buying rubber and ivory; weeding lawns on Cape Cod, I conjured images of searching for rare jungle plants.

Staring into the rushing water, I recall a few eyewitness accounts of Mokele-Mbembe. The Pygmies who live near Lake Télé agree that the god-beast has blood-red eyes and rust-colored skin covered with a short, napped fur. It has a long, slender neck and an equally long tail. Inside its giant mouth is one lone tooth, a jumbo tusk that can easily puncture a crocodile squama. The Pygmies have told outsiders that the god-beast is as long as a row of elephants and taller than two elephants stacked up. A professional hunter based in Djéké, a village not far from Lake Télé, told officials that Mokele-Mbembe is only a little larger than a hippopotamus, with a neck as long as its body. Its tracks, according to Alfred A. Smith, better known as Trader Horn, are the size of cheese wheels.

It's possible that these reports have been exaggerated. The paleontologists I sought out in preparation for this search dismissed the notion of a living sauropod, but with a wink one admitted that the experts have been wrong in the past. Much of the land around Lake Télé is unexplored, and as Harvard professor Deane Bowers told me, "Who knows what's out there? We have models that tell us what's probable, but surprising discoveries are made every day."

I'm distracted from my musings by a light bobbing along the opposite shore, nearly a half-mile away in Zaire. Someone appears to be jumping from rock to rock with a lantern in hand. During the daylight hours, people prowl the shores of the rapids, scavenging for fish and useful debris marooned by the surging waters, but even then it's risky business. The light vanishes abruptly. Instinctively I press myself tight against the rock.

Four miles upstream the wharf lamps of central Brazzaville illumine the right bank, and those of Kinshasa spill out from the left bank. The upper floors of the deluxe hotels are easy to spot, as are the ferry port lights, which cast a pinkish glow onto Stanley Pool. From where I sit, high above the torrent, it's hardly imaginable that beyond the rapids a mile from here, the Congo River meanders peacefully, entirely navigable for a thousand miles.

Charged with the power of the river, I turn back to the nightclub. The band is on a break, and scores of people are milling about the parking area. Cars with sound systems are surrounded by finger-snapping revelers; couples pair off and stroll hand in hand into the night; groups of men flirt with women walking by. As I emerge from the darkness, people stare and whisper. Perhaps I do look a bit odd, lumbering out of the bush, a sodden apparition, with squeaking shoes and a bare head reflecting the green neon. Someone kindly asks if I need a doctor.

Surely Ambroise is still here somewhere, I think, spotting the taxi and working my way toward the club entrance. Two soldiers snap to attention as I pass their jeep. Their Chinese-made AK-47s swing into a ready position.

"Halte-là!" one of them orders as his partner flips on the headlights. The taller of the two men directs me into the high beams, indicating a spot with his rifle.

"Quel est le problème?" I ask.

The lanky corporal starts talking in a mixture of French, Lingala, and some other dialect. I ask him to slow down, explaining that I'm an American tourist. This only irritates him, and he speaks faster.

"Caporal, s'il vous plaît, plus lentement?"

He grunts, resumes speed, and speaks louder, as if that will help drive home his words. Since Americans have until recently been barred from visiting the People's Republic of the Congo, this may be his first opportunity to lecture one. He clearly regards me as part of a menacing culture. Americans, he says, are devils in the service of Henry Kissinger, Satan himself. I fish out my passport and visas, which are damp but not ruined; he passes them to his sidekick and presses on. His many hours with the Red Book are evident as he peppers his lecture with many of the Great Helmsman's flowery phrases. The thoughtful Beijing embassy stocks bookstores with copies free of charge.

"Trouble?" a voice asks to my left. It's Ambroise. He flashes his identification, takes my passport, and asks the soldiers what I've done wrong. Assured that they are only checking my papers, Ambroise takes charge and tells them, "Don't worry. I know how to handle him."

Ambroise motions for me to back off while he confers with the soldiers. He jots something on a piece of paper, hands it to the corporal, and with a laugh whisks me along to the taxi.

"I gave the soldier the name of your hotel. You should expect to see him one of these days. He wants to discuss the revolution with you."

"Thanks, pal."

"De rien."

The four doors of the taxi are swung wide open. The cabbie is stretched across the back seat looking for coins. Up front, Reuben spins the dial of the tinny radio, cursing with the flair of a longshoreman. He can't locate his favorite station. The crew from the Palm Club is also there, and Ambroise tells how he has just rescued me from a night in jail, referring to himself as my "hero."

The hack decides to go back to work, and I grab a ride, content with my night and anxious to have a pillow under my head while the river images are fresh.

"Did you fall in?" the cabbie asks, eyeing my wet shirt.

"In a way I suppose I did."

"They told me you were looking for a dinosaur."

"Yes . . . Mokele-Mbembe."

"Are you crazy?"

"Not really."

"When I was young, my mother told me about Mokele-Mbembe, but I never believed her."

"C'est dommage!" I say, confident that Saint George missed a few dragons, and grateful for all my dinosaur dreams.

CHAPTER ◆ 3

THE DAWN SKY is a dull terra cotta, threatening rain. The meteorologist on TV Zaire appears at irregular intervals and makes broad, vague predictions: nice, not so nice, not nice at all. The Congo's largest newspaper, *Mweti*, publishes an almanac and a star guide, but the most recent "Night Sky" column mapped the heavens only above 50 degrees north latitude. While this might be useful for travelers flying to Paris, it's hardly practical for those of us grounded in Brazzaville. Paris, once the center of the colonial universe, still casts a long shadow.

Since the Congo straddles the equator, Brazzaville is never far from the sun's zenith; and twice a year it is directly overhead. This makes predicting the temperature a snap. During the day it's usually in the high eighties, and it rarely drops more than eighteen degrees at night. The humidity hovers constantly between 80 and 100 percent. Most people carry an umbrella all the time.

Today, with my scheduled appointment with the minister, I'm full of optimism. Finally I'll be able to shove off for Lake Télé.

"A thousand francs says it will rain before you get to the Ministry of Forests," Robert wagers from across the table. He's ostensibly the hotel manager, but there's no mistaking that it's his mother who is in charge. He dangles a bank note in the air.

Every morning we drink coffee together in the hotel garden, smoking Gauloises and reading yesterday's news from Paris. Sensing that this is my lucky day and sure that it won't rain before noon, I up the ante.

"Make that two thousand, and you're on."

Robert drops the bills into the Limoges sugar pot. "Safe as a bank," he assures me, replacing the lid.

The staff has strict orders not to touch the porcelain his parents brought to the Congo from France after World War II. His mother cherishes every cup, saucer, and plate; it was all she managed to salvage from their bombed-out home. Hoping to start a new life far from the aching reminders of war, his parents were part of a wave of French émigrés, many of whom first visited the Congo when Brazzaville was de Gaulle's headquarters. Today some 35,000 French citizens live in the Congo; they represent less than two percent of the population, but they control most of the economy.

The Ministry of Forests is several miles from the hotel, and Robert offers to show me a shortcut. He draws a map on a napkin. The confusing hatchmarks that look to be slips of his pen are actually bus routes. There's no direct bus, and I'm instructed to make two transfers. Brazzaville's roads and transit system, Robert says, were designed years ago by colonial engineers fond of curves.

"We French savor the indirect approach, but you know, it's usually the quickest way to get what you want."

In the past I've walked to the ministry, but I don't want to arrive sweaty for this morning's rendezvous. In theory I could take a taxi, but in practice I can't afford one. There are no meters, so haggling determines the fare. Unable to speak fluent French or Lingala, I'm fair game when not traveling with Ambroise. My Berlitz phrase book is woefully inadequate for such situations: "I don't want to dance anymore" has yet to help my bargaining position.

I arrive at the Congo Pharmacy depot just as the bus pulls in, and I hop aboard. The lemon-yellow plastic seats are all occupied, so I stand facing a political placard that reads: "You are special! You are the Congo! Celebrate, after work of course!" The Renault bus, with its untuned engine belching smoke, rumbles around the rotary and heads up Rue de Docteur Jannot.

The bus driver hands me a transfer ticket and drops me off at an unmarked street corner. Just as I step from the bus a thunderclap explodes, and rain starts pouring down. Lightning streaks the horizon with a speed matched only by that of Robert's fingers dipping into the sugar pot for his winnings. One of the other commuters, an older man with blackened teeth, offers me a spot under his umbrella.

"Are you thirsty, young man?" He thumps his briefcase. "My spirits can cure your problems."

My confused look speaks for me. I know that witch doctors make house calls to banish lurking devils, but hawking remedies on the street is a new one.

"Come closer," he invites, glancing about and making sure none of the other commuters can see.

"Ah," I exclaim, looking at his cache. The briefcase is filled with an array of corked liquor bottles. He snaps the case shut as my hand reaches out.

"You are embassy staff, yes?"

"No, a tourist — American."

"Merde. I should have known . . . the shoes, the shoes . . ."

I'm wearing my best outfit for the meeting with the deputy minister. My pants are a bit wrinkled, but they're clean; my shirt is pressed; my green clip-on tie is perfectly knotted; my shoes have new laces and a fresh shine.

"What's wrong with my shoes?"

"Nothing, nothing at all," he says forlornly. "But I should have known that you weren't Russian . . . The toe is too pointy."

Marin, the moonshiner, is headed to a conference of Eastern Bloc engineers to peddle his hooch. Last year the Russian embassy began to curb the number of bottles its staff could officially procure each month, so Marin seized the opportunity to profit.

"I sell the briefcase. What's inside is free," he says with a smirk.

The rain continues as we huddle under the umbrella. Puddles have grown into pools, and the gutter has been transformed into a sluiceway, cluttered with the flotsam and jetsam of everyday city life.

"Where does it all go?" I wonder aloud.

"Zaire," Marin pipes so all can hear. "All the shit goes to Zaire, oui?"

The other people at the bus stop nod their heads in agreement. Zaire bashing is common among the Congolese, but it doesn't seem particularly malicious. Both sides of the river are steeped in a common heritage of language, music, dance, religion, and tribal traditions. Both were once part of the Kongo Kingdom, a Bantu nation that stretched northward to Gabon and south as far as Angola. Internecine wars had already fragmented the kingdom before the Europeans arrived and started underwriting the conflicts in order to consolidate their own power and ensure a steady supply of slaves. Come independence in the 1960s, the two countries went in opposite political directions, but the cultural ties have remained unbroken. From what I've observed, Zairese and Congolese regard each other as cousins, and like cousins, they poke fun at each other as often as they express sympathy.

"We don't have much," one woman says, casting a rueful glance toward Kinshasa, "but they have less."

The bus screeches to a halt and we climb aboard. Marin grabs the seat next to me, tilting his umbrella in such a way that one of my cuffs fills with water. Apologizing profusely, he offers to make amends with some black-market bargains. As we slow to a stop at the transfer station, the bus to the ministry pulls up right behind us. "Quelle chance!" he exclaims.

"You're right," I reply, taking this as another good omen. In just a few days, I think, I'll be slashing my way down jungle trails tracking a dinosaur.

The Ministry of Forests is housed in a five-story building as solid and uninspired as a military bunker. The windows are stark vertical slots in the cement façade, which, wet from rain, is the color of coal ash. Piles of concrete blocks lie helterskelter about the grounds, suggesting that a perimeter wall may have been part of the original design. Turning a corner of the building, I steer around a thick copper wire running off the roof and into a puddle. When the sky crackles, I bolt for the door.

In the lobby neither guards nor receptionists are in sight. The official directory indicates a high turnover rate: one column lists job titles in a neat sign painter's hand, the other has names and office numbers written in chalk. An eraser hangs by a string at the bottom of the directory.

I find the deputy minister's office number and head up the stairs.

"Hey, wait for me," a familiar voice echoes up the stairway.

Ambroise climbs slowly, leaning heavily on the handrail. His eyelids droop, his shoulders slump. Yes, he stayed at the nightclub until it closed.

Like every other office I've visited in the Congo, the deputy minister's is chock-a-block with well-worn furniture. The guiding principle seems to be the more of everything the better. The ceiling is layered with swatches of batik fabric, and the walls are covered with photographs, blowups from ministry pamphlets. In one a colossal log skidder drags a bundle of trees up a steep incline; in another two men wearing hardhats wield chain saws at the base of an ancient djave nut tree; along the far wall is a sequence of photographs documenting the various stages of lumbering, from cutting to loading milled planks aboard ships. Obviously, international concerns about the rain forest have yet to affect this office. Only petroleum generates more export revenue for the Congo than timber, and the government, operating under a Russian model, has developed an ambitious five-year plan to cut and sell its natural wealth.

I swallow my personal suggestions on conservation and resource management.

"Please, sit," the secretary tells me. My pacing seems to make him nervous.

I ease into a club chair with brown horsehair poking through the crazed Naugahyde. Across the aisle, stretched out on a three-cushion sofa, Ambroise wrestles with Morpheus. At ten o'clock I remind the secretary of my nine o'clock appointment.

"I know. The minister knows . . . Soon, monsieur, soon," he says, continuing to clean his typewriter.

Two more hours crawl by, and I ask whether I should return tomorrow.

"Stay," he advises, working a toothbrush in under the platen. "I know. The minister knows."

Past experience has taught me to carry a thick book when visiting government offices; I return to my book as Ambroise attempts to read an issue of *Timber Industry* with his eyes closed. The secretary's typewriter is now the cleanest Olivetti in the Congo. Another hour passes.

"Is the minister here today?" No one, I realize, has gone in
or out of the private office.

"Oh, he is not away."

"Is he in the building?"

"Soon, monsieur, soon," chirps the loyal liege.

"Soon?"

"Soon means soon, oui?"

"Certainement," I concede.

Thirty minutes later Ambroise rousts himself. His escort duty comes on top of his normal work load, and he must visit his own office. "Writing a proposal for toilets in Lengoué village might actually wake me up," he says, shuffling out the door. I promise to call him before leaving the building.

By now I'm positive that the minister isn't in, but it's important to stick it out just in case he returns today. No one is going to hand over a permit simply because I've emptied my bank account to visit Mokele-Mbembe. Securing a travel permit is my job at the moment, and waiting is part of the workday.

Of course, the fact that I'm looking for a dinosaur probably doesn't help. Somehow I have to convince the skeptics that my proposal is a worthy venture. I need to remind those in power of an earlier, simpler time in their lives when they, too, spent afternoons imagining themselves plunging into the jungle after some legendary beast.

I finish my book and kill the remaining hours helping the secretary fix another old typewriter. We manage to make the F key work again with a paper clip bent just the right way. The secretary tests our repair by writing a memo to his boss, suggesting that my appointment be rescheduled within a few days.

"Thanks."

"Yeah, sure," he replies, adding, "There are three more typewriters that need work. We'll fix them all when you return."

As he locks the door, he shrugs his shoulders and checks his watch. "You waited nine hours. C'est la vie, eh?"

"Oui, c'est la vie," I concur and lead him to the café across the street. The espressos are on me.

The deputy minister is in no hurry to reschedule our meeting but, undeterred, I maintain my routine, visiting various government offices Monday through Friday. Simple persistence earns me a modicum of respect and, more important, several friendships among the office workers. They greet me warmly now, and occasionally one will ask me to join them for lunch.

My embroidered knowledge of American heroes, fictive and real, is a primary asset. What happens to J. R. Ewing and Hoss in upcoming shows is valuable information. And there can never be enough talk about Muhammad Ali. His 1974 bout with George Foreman, the "Rumble in the Jungle" held in Kinshasa, is still a frequent topic. It's not unusual to meet someone who has memorized the radio broadcast and will, without prompting, reenact every feint, jab, and rope-a-dope maneuver. Since I once shook hands with Ali on a New York street corner, I'm accorded undeserved respect. My description of the meeting has been embellished as it circulates through the bureaucracy, and if people believe that I've sparred with Ali, as Ambroise now suggests, that's fine by me.

CHAPTER ◆ 4

R EMEMBER THE MARTYRS of the revolution," a red sign on the side of a store admonishes. Directly below it are dozens of fliers advertising a sale on Levi's: "All sizes! All colors!" Several blocks away the ambiguities of a socialist state fed by a free market economy are even more evident. The hammer and sickle flutters above the ultramodern, privately owned Score Supermarket. In its windows the advertisements for the daily specials are suffixed with cautionary notes from the government: "Freedom is never on sale" and "Every day we step closer to the ideal, comrades."

"Party officials ask us to do it," the owner of a Mercedes dealership tells me, nodding to a Maoist aphorism on the wall of his showroom. "I'm a capitalist," he said unapologetically. "And my best customers are generals and politicians . . . They're always trading up."

On the front page of this morning's newspaper is an article about the government's latest enticement to French multinational companies. Next to it is a lengthy story about the erection of another statue dedicated to those who died battling imperialism. I show the paper to Robert, the hotelier, as we drink coffee.

"The real question is where are they going to put the statue?" he says. "I don't think there's any room left."

Heroic sculptures stand in the center of most city rotaries and on the busier street corners. During the twenty-minute walk from the hotel to Ambroise's office, I pass nine monuments to the revolution.

Ambroise is standing outside his office building and once again bars me from seeing his office. Today, he says, it's too nice to go indoors; yesterday it was too muggy. I wonder if he has something to hide, a dart board, perhaps, with my picture on it.

"How did you know?" he quips. He asks for a cigarette, takes several long drags, and says, "Well, it's over. New orders came today, and we're free of each other . . . This shadow disappears."

"Comment?"

"I'm no longer your escort." He declines to explain why, and I don't press the issue, but both of us are delighted with this new development. We make plans for a celebratory drink later at the Palm Club, and as we go our separate ways for the first time in three weeks, I feel a sense of relief.

The escort detail disrupted life for both of us, as Ambroise mentioned at least twice a day. Ambroise loathed my afternoon constitutional, cursing the birds I watched, tapping his foot impatiently as I gathered seeds and cuttings. Now that he's gone, I can go wherever I want.

Downtown has little that interests me, so I head east across the Plateau district, the city center, which spreads out over the high, flat ground facing the river. I trudge past numerous government offices, hotels, embassies, and tall bank towers that wouldn't be out of place in Zurich.

In the Chad district the streets become shady avenues lined with spacious houses built for the colonial gentry in the early 1900s. Along every street, construction crews are at work building walls around the houses. Brazzaville has one of the lowest crime rates of any city in Africa, but still the walls are going up.

"When you have more than you need, I guess you scare easy," one mason tells me as he cements jagged glass atop an eight-foot wall. He pauses for a moment, eyes a hunk of broken green glass, and says, "When I get rich, I'm going to have dogs and electric fences. Anyone can climb over these stupid walls."

I pick up the pace when I spot smokestacks, the spires of industry, that prod the sky above the Plaine district, a lowland area jammed with one-story factories, warehouses, and docks. On windless days like today, the factories are veiled by a sooty fog and appear pressed to the ground. Even so, the Plaine appeals to me; it's the heart of the black market and has a dark seam running through it that I find attractive.

This industrial district manufactures a dizzying array of sounds, from the dull rhythmic thumping of hydraulic presses to the high, quick music of spinning ball bearings. Forklifts race along the streets, and cranes swing their arms overhead. Near the water, human chains snake up and around corners, loading and unloading the river barges. Six hundred thousand tons of goods pass through the port yearly. There's always work, but the pay, I'm told by one weary longshoreman, is "just enough to keep me from returning to my village."

A whistle sounds lunch break, and the Plaine grows quiet. I sit on the tong of a forklift, eating an orange, and watch painters and sculptors set up their artwork along warehouse walls.

"Cheap. Good and cheap," one artist shouts, pointing to a large canvas.

"Is that a . . ." I flip through my Bantam French/English dictionary. "Found it . . . Is that a pagoda?"

"Oui. It is very Chinese, don't you agree?"

I certainly won't argue; there are plenty of swirls before pines and several pagodas.

The artist introduces himself, "Marcel Cedan."

He asks for a slice of my orange and then for a cigarette.

"Only you foreigners buy; Congolese don't look twice . . . This painting is for embassy people."

Art for art's sake is all but unknown in the Congo. The traditional culture subordinates beauty to practicality and relegates all creative work to religious contexts, particularly the spiritual imagery used by witch doctors.

"It's all craft. Art is nowhere." Marcel complains. He wants to return to Paris, where he studied painting on a grant from the Communist Workers Party. He takes another cigarette, tips his beret, and trots off.

"Sir! Sir! Beautiful pagodas on sale . . . Memories of home! Right here," he calls, linking arms with a passing Chinese diplomat. "Come with me, the great Marcel . . ."

After lunch the forklifts and the lumpers return to their drudgery, and the artists retreat to a café several blocks from the riverfront. The dock area hums until six o'clock, quitting time. Come dark, an eerie silence pervades the area, dogging anyone walking its shadowy alleys and empty streets.

Refreshed by a triple espresso at a local café, I set off down a narrow street festooned with clotheslines. If there are zoning laws in Brazzaville, they're not enforced in this neighborhood. Warehouses bash up against tenements, which lean upon garages, which abut small shops, all the structures slanting one way or another. The street bleeds into the staging area for the Kinshasa ferry, and I wade through a crush of people jockeying for a place in line. The sloping macadam before me is clogged with taxis, trucks, and pedestrians. Off to my left, sitting in the shade of a eucalyptus tree, is a lone soldier, his body slumped in defeat. Two or three women are yelling at him, demanding that he "do something about this mess." Pushcart operators elbow and curse their way to the boats. Taxi drivers play cards or hustle customers; all of them have left their engines idling, filling the air with exhaust fumes. Tea vendors compete with coffee sellers, and a shaved-ice salesman accuses a lemonade dealer of selling diuretics. Cigarette vendors hawk individual smokes from opened Marlboro packs; a young boy carrying a pocket lighter follows each tobacco peddler, yelling out, "Two francs . . . two francs a light."

Down the street, across from Ho Garden, a North Vietnamese restaurant, money changers bark exchange rates that fluctuate from breath to breath. People line up to convert their Congolese francs into makutas and zaires. In the shade of cardboard awnings, fishmongers fillet atop jury-rigged tables made from plastic milk boxes.

"Mister American, buy?" a boy entreats, holding out a smelly perch covered in flies.

An army truck lumbers into the area and disgorges a platoon of soldiers. Armed with automatic rifles, they march grinning through the crowd, scattering people like chickens. Lookouts for the illegal money changers whistle the warning: "Whirl-a-who . . . whirl-a-who."

I move on to the railway station north of here, at the edge of Poto-Poto, aptly named after the Nigerian pidgin for mud. The entire district sits on swampland, and whenever the rain comes, the area becomes a slough. The first French colonists gave this land to the Senegalese mercenaries they lured away from the English in Nigeria. Over the years Poto-Poto has grown into a sprawl of hovels, but the government is now replacing many of the shanties with small brick houses. A sign on one construction site announces "the birth of a splendid Poto-Poto."

As I stroll its muddy streets, I hear people chattering around me, trying to determine whether I'm lost *(perdu)*; daffy *(toqué)*; or an international relief worker *(homme avec francs)*. When a gaggle of youngsters rolling a moped tire spot me, they let the tire flop to the ground. Jaws drop, eyes pop open. After a few seconds, one boy manages to speak.

"Na-na-n'wambi," he stutters, naming a spirit known for its pale complexion, and the gang bolts.

N'wambis aren't considered evil, but folklore advises having as little contact with them as possible. They're displaced spirits, forced out into the open whenever a building is demolished, burned, or refurbished. They wander about their old neighborhoods searching for a comfortable corner or doorway to inhabit.

I jump aboard the first bus heading out of Poto-Poto toward the opposite end of town, the Bacongo district. It's the most populous section of Brazzaville and my favorite. The fourth bus I board drops me off in front of the Bacongo peanut market, which spreads out over an entire city block. Each stall is roofed with long sheets of colored plastic that billow in the slightest breeze, and under the plastic, vendors hunch over skillets the size of manhole covers, roasting nuts, adding honey and spices according to family recipes. Apollinaire, the owner of City Nuts, asks me to taste peanuts glazed in pineapple and lemon juice. We both agree the recipe needs some fine tuning.

Nearby is a shoe market offering a wide array of footwear, from Italian high heels to sandals made from old tires. Cobblers spit tacks while they talk, and treadle sewing machines thump-a-thump as soles are stitched into place.

Most of the stands in the vegetable market sell a single product: one stand sells only coconuts, another only mangoes. Today I buy a few slices of pineapple from Claude and Marie. Only European-style supermarkets with refrigerators can offer a variety of produce, Claude explains. In this heat, and with the clouds of insects, green pineapples ripen overnight and rot within days. He checks with the other dealers on his block before he goes to the wholesale market, making sure that whatever he buys isn't already on somebody else's shelf.

"If we had to compete with each other, we'd go broke in a couple of days," he adds.

I pass up Claude's offer of a mashed-banana lunch and wander down the street to the People's Diner, run by Marie-Joseph, whom Ambroise introduced to me weeks ago. A large woman who describes herself as "a hundred kilos of love," she cooks under the raised hood of a truck, bending over a kerosene stove balanced on the engine. The menu is painted on the door of the truck, and I order the Congo stew.

"We must fatten you up," Marie-Joseph purrs, ladling a hefty portion into a wooden salad bowl. The next customer is served his meal in an institution-size mayonnaise jar.

The stew meat is stringy but sweet. "What's this?" I ask, spooning a chunk of the meat.

"It's good, that's what it is." Marie-Joseph scoops seconds into my bowl.

"It's delicious, but what kind of meat?"

"Rabbit or crow . . . I ran out of rabbit when this good-looking boy came by selling crows."

Several blocks closer to the river are several streets of clothing stores, a few with the latest fashions from Paris and New York. A theater marquee advertises noon to midnight showings of a Bruce Lee movie. Future ninja stars practice their kicks as they stand in line for tickets. A little farther on is a cluster of beauty salons, and freshly coiffured women pause conspicuously as they pass store windows to check their reflection.

Ambroise has showed me a shortcut to the rapids through backyards and empty lots. As I walk along the footpath I nod to women tending cookfires in kitchen areas set up in lean-tos behind their homes. They nod back, a welcome reception in contrast to the baleful stares they gave me when I first passed through here. Toddlers still run for cover, however. A gang of teenagers playing soccer in an empty lot always exacts a toll from me. Several days ago they demanded a thousand francs but settled for a Polaroid group shot.

"Again, mister, again," they shout, wanting another photograph. I'm happy to oblige.

A few minutes later, as I approach the rapids, my body relaxes, and I exhale contentedly as I take a seat atop "my" rock, a granite boulder polished by eons of swift-running water. There's no telling when a wave will leap up and smack me, so I've left my camera bag behind, hooked to an African oak.

In India or Tibet it's not unusual to see a lama meditating beside a stream, the sound of water his mantra. The lessons I have learned from Himalayan mystics come into play as I stare into the swirl of the rapids. I reach out to make contact with Mokele-Mbembe through the river. The water relieves my mind of nagging thoughts of bureaucratic hassles and of my ever-flattening wallet. It's just Mokele-Mbembe and me, the water delivering my messages into the jungle.

Most Congolese believe in one supreme deity, the Creator, but even the most powerful witch doctors don't pray directly to the god of gods. The Creator is far removed from earthly happenings and beyond human comprehension. Instead, the appeals are directed toward lesser gods, such as the spirits of the water, air, and forest. These gods, who interact on the same plane as mankind, are accessible, I'm told, and respond to the same enticements people do: prostration, persistence, and bribery.

"Promise the gods something in return for your permit," Ambroise once advised. "If you want something, give something . . . Make offerings."

I'm willing to try anything. Before leaving the rapids, I always toss a piece of fruit into the river. Today it's pineapple.

CHAPTER ◆ 5

C OME BACK TOMORROW," the ministry official says in
farewell, ending a fifty-second meeting that was scheduled to begin four hours and twelve minutes ago.

My dour mood brightens outside the office building as a
West African river eagle glides over me, its wings fully extended. Blue-naped mousebirds scurry along the limbs of a
tulip tree, and a pair of mustached scrub warblers frolic in a
hedge. I decide to cancel lunch with the American consul and
spend the rest of the day birding.

The best birding spots, far from downtown, are in the hills
beyond the Chad district and north of the cemetery. Recently
I've been tracking a pair of hammerkops, *Scopus umbretta*,
which live on the right bank of the Foa, a small stream that
eventually empties into Stanley Pool. Standing nearly two feet
high, these birds derive their name from a crest that projects

in opposition to their long, curved bills, giving them the profile of a claw hammer. They are dull brown in color, and their call is an unsatisfying shrill piping, but their nests are the mansions of the avian world. Relentless builders, they spend hours each day gathering suitable debris to expand their homes. The nest I've been observing could accommodate an entire flock of swallows. A massive weave of twigs and grass, it has a thick floor, rounded corners, a sloping roof, and a small, ovate entrance.

Among the items I brought with me from America are a gross of psychedelic-colored pencils with rainbow leads. Children will love these, I thought back in New York, but I was wrong; they pester me instead for money or cigarettes. Perhaps the hammerkops will like them. I place four pencils on a castor oil bush and conceal myself. Within an hour, each pencil has been carried aloft and become part of the hammerkop's roof.

Come dusk the birds leave their manse to prowl the stream. I trail the female as she stalks frogs, cockeyed and bending into the wind. As the sun dips below the treetops, the bird takes off, flapping her wings madly, raising a gust of air that carries her scent of mildewed towel to me. In flight, the hammerkop bobs and dips awkwardly. I chase after her, keeping a safe distance and stopping when she lands near a small pool of stagnant water far from the stream.

"Rivet . . . rivet," a bold frog calls, sounding its own death knell.

Above me the fiery sky is rapidly burning out. Mosquitoes have begun to swarm, and cicadas loose their monotonous mating calls. To the north I can hear the chatter of monkeys. They sound excited, as if they've seen a snake. Snake! The thought chills me, and I scout the ground nearby. All clear.

"Rivet . . . rivet."

The frog has yet to notice the tiptoeing predator and continues to call. The bird moves noiselessly.

Twack! The hammerkop strikes, her bill neatly skewering the frog.

At the other end of the pool there's another "rivet . . . rivet," and the hammerkop swings her head toward dessert. She walks cautiously, stopping every few steps to scrutinize the area. I'm on my belly, flat to the ground and inching backward, away from her path. The bird keeps coming. Only twenty feet separate us.

Crunch . . . snap . . . crunch. Dozens of seedpods crackle as I back under a tree. The hammerkop flies away, whistling derisively.

Angry at having disturbed her, I slap the tree trunk, smearing my hand with a sticky resin. I look up, and towering over me is the broad umbrella crown of a flame tree *(Delonix regia)*. Most of its scarlet flowers have passed, though a few stubborn survivors remain, dangling like small red bells in the flush of new leaves. The tiny leaflets have twisted their stems, searching for what light remains. As it darkens, the leaves seem to droop; but then, beginning at the base of each limb and radiating outward, in quick succession each of the thousands of leaflets curls up for the night, awaiting dawn reveille before opening again.

In no time it's pitch black and I head back to my rendezvous with Ambroise at the Palm Club. Downtown is to the southeast, four to six miles away, I guess; my flair for disorientation rules out certainty. Having learned how to navigate aboard a boat, where abstraction (such as lowering the heavens to gain an earthly fix) is an integral part of plotting, I find it easy to become lost on land.

Not sure about the correct path to Ambroise and a cold beer, I tramp off in the direction of the Fly, a busy cluster of stars on the southern horizon. This far from the city, I've got company every step of the way. Wild dogs shadow my movements, yelping as they rustle through the tall grass. Night is when most predators and scavengers emerge, and I check the slingshot in my camera bag. My first line of defense, though, will be a lively rendition of George Thorogood's hit, "Bad to the Bone."

I've walked for a half-hour when I see the flickering of a campfire ahead. Keeping my flashlight pointed down, away from my face, I stage a noisy approach.

"Hello? Bonsoir? . . ." I shout.

"Fiche-moi le camp!" someone shouts. I discern the silhouette of a tall man standing and another person sitting.

"I'm lost and . . ."

"Beat it!" the man repeats. I turn, ready to chase the Fly again.

"Aidez-lui, Jean," a soft voice intercedes.

The man grumbles loudly and jabs a stick into the fire. Orange cinders swirl, and the breeze lifts a few tiny fireballs toward Hydra.

"Where do you want to go?"

"The city . . . Bacongo district."

"Tokay," he yells, bounding off.

"Tokay" is Lingala for "let's go," and I chug after him. He stays five yards ahead of me, moving swiftly through the knee-high savanna grass. The moon isn't up yet, and my flashlight is useless at such a pace. The terrain becomes hilly, yet my guide lopes along with graceful strides, at ease with the night and the land. He moves instinctively, shifting this way and that in some unwavering connection to the earth. We weave onward, never slackening the pace, and I begin to wonder if he's pouring on the steam to test me. Somehow I keep up, and despite myself I lock into his rhythm.

I got my first lessons in tropical navigation nearly ten years ago in Nicaragua. My teacher was a man named Nando, whom most people called the Jaguar in honor of his fighting skills. Somoza's army offered a large reward for his capture, but he escaped every trap. Nando showed me how to find the best route by lying down and sighting along animal paths. At the eye level of a pangolin it became clear that zigzag routes are purposeful, each turn and shift a reflection of a topographical nuance. To avoid tiring, animals keep angling this way and that, compensating for rises and dips in the landscape:

"People may be dumb or smart, practical or not," Nando observed. "Animals, my Yankee friend, are rarely smart, but they are always practical."

My guide tonight offers no such comforting insights, maintaining a stony silence until we reach the railroad tracks. He hasn't looked straight at me once.

"Suivez le chemin de fer."

"Merci."

"You are quite welcome," he replies in perfect English and disappears silently into the bush.

The tracks run from Brazzaville to Pointe-Noire, the Congo's ocean port and second largest city, 318 miles away. The Congo-Ocean Railroad, completed in 1934 by the French, incorporates ninety bridges and twelve tunnels, including one, Africa's longest, through Mount Bamba. While rummaging through the records of the project in the National Archives, I found one brochure that called the railroad "a miracle in railroad history . . . French genius at work." Another extolled the tracks as a conduit that "would bring civilization into the heart of savage Africa."

Last week, hearing that the minister was going to Pointe-Noire for a few days, I, too, planned an outing to the coast, booking a room in the same hotel as the minister. He took a plane, but I decided on the train. When I arrived at the depot, however, the platform was empty, although the train was due to leave in a few minutes. The old iron horse just sat there.

"Excuse me," I asked a railway employee. "Is there a delay?"

"A day or two, possibly three."

Pierre, the stationmaster, introduced himself and offered me coffee. "Come to my office."

He led me behind stacks of burlap-wrapped bundles, old suitcases, and wooden crates to a small mahogany-paneled room with the initials of two generations of railway workers carved in the dark wood. Pictures of trains were tacked on the walls, and the floor was covered with piles of yellow paper. The three clocks on the wall each displayed a different time.

"This climate is hell on machines . . . The military has priority on parts. It may be three days before passengers ride again," he explained, scooping five teaspoons of sugar into his cup.

With my trip scrubbed and his day unburdened by any schedule, I settled in for a morning of stories from a man who had three loves: "God. Family. Railroads." He was genuinely pleased to answer my questions, as his children and grandchildren had tired of his tales. "How can an old man compete with television?" he asked.

I listened spellbound to grim anecdotes about the construction of the railroad that were omitted from the records in the National Archives. Laborers were collected by French Légionnaires and mercenaries who roamed the countryside, rounding up all males over the age of fifteen. The natives were, by law, commanded to render one week of free service to the state each year, so a twenty-year-old was indentured for twenty weeks of labor at wages that never covered the cost of food at the company stores. Those who tried to escape were whipped or hanged.

In the archives, the reports of the chief medical officer stated that in 1927, the worst year, 60 percent of the black work force died on the job. Malaria was listed as the most common cause of death. Over the course of the project, from 1920 to 1934, the official records listed 17,000 deaths.

"That, my friend, is a lie . . . French whitewash," the stationmaster said. "At least 30,000 died building the railroad." That would be 93 bodies for every mile of track, making this the bloodiest railroad ever built.

"My great-uncle died with his feet off the ground," the stationmaster said, showing me pictures of nearly naked chain gangs. Somewhere in each picture was a gallows with a hangman's noose suspended from a crosstree, and a white man holding a gun. In this humidity the guillotine couldn't operate smoothly, so the managers set up a gallows in each work camp, cynically charging construction and maintenance costs to the Colonial Education Department. After all, the gallows were teaching devices built for the edification of the workers.

"It was a mean-spirited time." the stationmaster mused, putting the photographs away and closing the drawer on a benighted colonial period.

◆

Thoughts about my morning with the stationmaster fade after a mile of walking down the tracks toward the Palm Club. It's a beautiful night, with a waning moon sneaking above the horizon and moving slowly toward Sirius in the constellation of the Big Dog. Curlews punctuate the night air with their signature call: "Coo-loo . . . coo-loo." I call back softly, but the curlews fall silent.

My mood darkens as I see, just off to the left of the tracks, a mangled, rusted structure that looks frighteningly like a man hanging by the neck. I start sprinting to escape the image, but specters seem to line the rails: every signal post a gallows, each mile marker a whipping post. I make it to the station in record time, bedraggled and willing to pay a cabbie whatever he wants to take me away.

"What happened to you? See a ghost or something?" Ambroise says as I enter the Palm Club. "Do yourself a favor and order a drink."

"You buying?" I turn my pockets inside out.

"Start a tab," Ambroise responds generously.

CHAPTER ◆ 6

IT'S SUNDAY and I'm going fishing. While Robert gets his boat from the marina, I wait at the ferry landing, guarding our cooler, three rods, and a bucket of live bait. The marina is no place for strangers, he told me. It's protected by snarling Dobermans caged between three rows of chain-link fencing. In the Congo more boats than cars are stolen, and one glance at the map explains why. The country has thousands of miles of navigable waterways and only 530 miles of paved roadway. There's a seven-month waiting list at the local Suzuki outboard-motor dealership, a frustration that causes many people to turn to the black market. Marin, the old moonshiner and fence, and my contact for illegal goods, says there are five maritime chop shops in the area for every one dealing in car parts. The Congolese navy is a barebones operation, with only two hundred men and officers, and Marin has never heard of them boarding a boat to inspect ownership papers.

As the rising sun bakes off the river fog, I slip into the shade of a giant kapok tree and wonder if the guard dogs mistook Robert for a snack. Travelers have used this particular tree as a landmark since long before Savorgnan de Brazza slept under it in 1879. Joseph Conrad and Roger Casement both refer to it in their logs; Trader Horn and Henry Stanley took compass bearings off its massive trunk; André Gide, Mary Kingsley, and Ivan Sanderson all noted it in their books.

From where I stand, there's an unobstructed view across Stanley Pool to the Kinshasa skyline, a wall of vertical geometric shapes. Above the tallest buildings, corporate logos seem to hover unsupported in the hot air. Skybooms hold aloft huge bundles of shimmering glass. They reflect not only the sun but Zaire's determination, no matter what the social and monetary cost, to be the cosmopolitan center of Africa. The cool glass and concrete high-rises offer a sharp backdrop to the lush, inviting serenity of the Pool.

Millions of years ago there was no river here; the entire Congo Basin, like the Amazon, was an arm of the ocean. Over time, as Africa collided with Eurasia, all outlets to the sea were dammed behind a mountainous rim of crystalline rock. A brackish lake formed, but eventually the water level rose and began spilling over the mountaintops. That original spillway is now the rapids, and Mokele-Mbembe may be the lone survivor of the prehistoric animal kingdom that once lapped the lake water.

Little more than a hundred years ago Kinshasa and Brazzaville were nothing more than the dreams of two men: Savorgnan de Brazza, who was hailed as the "Conscience of France," and Henry Stanley, a man who not only wrote his own press releases but believed them as well. It was near this kapok tree that Stanley envisioned the city King Leopold had charged him with establishing. He was infuriated to learn of de Brazza's treaty with King Makoko, chief of the Batekes, ceding to

France all land north of the lower Congo. Stanley swore he would found a city that would surpass anything the French could build. Today Kinshasa, the former Leopoldville, is a vast metropolis of three million, while Brazzaville has fewer than a half million residents.

For some reason the ferry linking the two cities isn't running today. Except for the two workmen cleaning windows at the terminal building, the staging area is empty. Pushcarts are chained to trees; taxi stands are vacant; flies and beetles have taken over the fish stands.

It's almost ten o'clock, and the birds' morning feeding frenzy is over; air traffic is reduced to the late-rising butterflies in search of brunch. A shoal of white *Beleonois aurota* fly by at knee level. These creamy beauties, with their three-inch wingspan, are among the largest members of the swallowtail family. They flit about excitedly, attracted by the urea-rich soil under the kapok tree; its historical significance hasn't kept dogs or people from peeing on it. A host of small whites from the Pieridae clan join the parade feasting near the trunk.

Out of the corner of my eye I see a flash of cobalt blue. Perhaps it's a *Papilio zalmaxis*, which would be the showpiece of my collection. I creep toward it on tiptoes, trying not to make a sound, a field guide in one hand and a telescoping net in the other.

"Qu'est-ce que vous faites là?" A voice calls out behind me. It's one of the men who has been washing the windows.

"Papillon . . . shh!" I say, pointing toward an empty spot on the ground. The big blue has gone.

"Oh," the workman sighs, shaking his head and walking away.

"Hey, why isn't the ferry running?"

He keeps walking away.

Glancing upstream, I spot a powerboat planing across the water. Its bow is riding high, and a mighty rooster tail is shooting up from the stern. Varoom! The boat is screaming along, yawing dangerously, on the thin line separating thrill from disaster. The craft skirts the tip of M'Bamou Island in the middle of the Pool and darts toward the ferry landing. The propeller whirrs as the boat hobbyhorses, the rails dipping with each untimely rudder movement. The man steering waves with both hands. It's Robert.

"She's a beauty, eh?" he calls out.

Staring at the muscle boat, all brawny engine in a deep-vee hull, I yearn for the sluggish safety of the ferry. The aft deck is an airfoil contoured to direct the wind through and around the engine. It resembles something Kookie would have drooled over on "77 Sunset Strip," with plenty of chrome on a spaghetti of exhaust pipes and manifolds. In fact, the design, power plant, and flaming red hull are vintage Americana, circa 1962. Where, I wonder, do photographers from *National Geographic* find all those dugout canoes to illustrate articles invariably entitled "Emerging Africa"?

"What took you so long?"

"I tried to gas up in Zaire, but the border is closed for the day. The Congress of Central African States is meeting in Brazzaville. Angola stuff," he says, referring to a five-nation summit called to mediate an end to the Angolan civil war.

"Are the Portuguese there?" From what I've been told by diplomats, any talks are doomed to failure without the Portuguese acting as brokers. Having been kicked out of Angola years ago, they're the only group without a hidden agenda.

But Robert isn't listening to me; he has fishing on the brain.

"Get in," he orders.

The boat surges forward, leaping from wave to wave, our wake curling toward the shore. This is my first boat ride on the Congo River, and it's not what I had imagined. In *Heart of Darkness*, Conrad described a voyage on the Congo as "like traveling back to the earliest beginnings of the world, when vegetation rioted on earth and big trees were kings. An empty stream, a great silence, an impenetrable forest." In a few minutes we've covered a distance that might have taken Conrad half a day to steam.

"Rewind your watch . . . It's 1986, not 1896," Robert sighs, decelerating and steering for Zaire.

Kinshasa's waterfront handles three times the tonnage of Brazzaville's, but many of the ships at the docks are listing rust-buckets. Sandwiched between a mothballed fleet of barges are hogged steamers and cannibalized tugs. Two paddle wheelers sit on the bottom, their rails used to tie off modern freighters. Speedboats armed with machine guns surround a luxury yacht; Robert says it belongs to President Mobutu Sese Seko.

We come abeam a wide boulevard, Trente Juin, that links downtown Kinshasa with the ritzy suburbs. To avoid seeing more of Africa than absolutely necessary, the Belgians built this avenue and lined it with European-style shops with quaint façades, invoking the architecture of old Brussels. Much of the strip was trashed during the riots of the sixties.

Close behind the waterfront warehouses stretch blocks of one-story buildings assembled from cardboard, wood scrap, and tarpaper, their roofs topped with billboards advertising beer, hernia belts, and hair products. "Shine like a star with Spray Sheen," says one sign depicting a couple with Milky Way hairdos.

What might have been forest twenty years ago has been swallowed by the urban tangle, a seemingly endless sprawl of decaying structures sliced through by narrow streets. Between 1970 and 1985 Kinshasa's population jumped eightfold, as two and a half million people left their farms for the city. Most are still waiting for the housing and jobs promised by President Mobutu.

In comparison to Kinshasa, Brazzaville seems tidy and open. Glancing at the right bank, I recall what André Gide wrote: "Brazzaville seems asleep, too big for its small activities."

Robert points to the far shore, where, he tells me, the Kongo Kingdom was founded by Nimi a Lukeni. Nimi, the son of a Bantu chief, left his village and, with a few other men, set up the Congo's first extortion racket, exacting tolls from anyone trying to cross the Pool. When his aunt refused to pay, Nimi killed her, breaking a most profound taboo. The tribe waited expectantly for the gods to strike him dead. When he was still alive several days later, Nimi informed the tribe that this was proof he was a god, because the gods don't kill other gods. In the same breath he appointed himself chief of the chiefs, leader of all Bantu tribes. Ruthless to those opposing his ascendency, he consolidated tribes and went on to guide a flourishing kingdom.

We reach Robert's secret fishing spot and drop anchor. Forested hills rise up from either bank, the remnants of once great pinnacles that have been humbled by eons of pounding rain. This section of the river, called the Corridor, rarely exceeds two miles in width. Above Ngabé, though, at the debouchure of the Kwa, the Congo is up to twelve miles wide in places. River islands, formed from silt and shifting currents through a process known as "braiding," dot the waterscape, though Ubangi folklore says they are actually stepping stones placed by the gods, who don't like to get their feet wet.

The Congo is the only major river in the world to flow on both sides of the equator, crossing it twice during its 2,710-mile run from Zambia to the Atlantic. Along its way, the river nearly boxes the compass, heading north from its headwaters and then west across the rain forest before angling south, through a series of twists and turns that confounded early geographers. On a map the river resembles a giant question mark.

Robert offers me two fishing rods. I take only one, explaining that in all the thousands of miles I've sailed trailing a hook off the stern, I've never once caught a fish. One rod is more than enough for me to handle.

Robert baits his line and casts. I peer into the bait bucket, which is filled with wriggling eels, eight inches long, with razorlike teeth.

"Never been bitten," Robert says, flashing all ten digits, and scoops an eel toward my feet.

Whap! I slam down my ever-handy field guide and stun the eel.

Robert heads aft with two poles; I move to the bow and lay out my notebook, field guides, and binoculars. With the engine off, I can hear the water lap the chine, sounding like so many wet kisses. There's no sign of other humanity except for the occasional Styrofoam cup floating by. It seems the river belongs to us today.

"Robert, where are we?"

"I'm not going to tell you." He will say only that the village of Maloukou-Tréchot is not far away. My map is about as informative as Robert. There are black location dots on either side of every name on the chart. Depending on which dot I use, Maloukou-Tréchot is either fifty-five or sixty-eight kilometers upriver from Brazzaville.

An osprey cruises effortlessly above us, its shadow cutting the water and jumping inside the boat. Downstream a flock of gull-billed terns laugh noisily. A quick look through the binoculars reveals birds in all directions: drongos, sunbirds, babblers, parrots. Robert belches in appreciation of this news and grabs another beer.

Off to port, about thirty yards away, kingfishers zip in and out of their nests in the soft mud bank. One is a shining blue kingfisher, the best diver of the Alcedinidae clan. Its hot colors — red and electric blue — pop in the sunlight as something upstream catches its eye. The bird makes a sudden turn, hovers, and dives, barely making a splash as it lances the water. It surfaces a few feet away, a river perch triumphantly clamped in its beak. Even Robert is impressed.

"Nice catch! . . . And look at all the prairies! The fish will be here soon."

Tiny islands, most the size of doormats, are floating down on our boat. The Congolese call these bits of detached riverbank prairies. Stands of reeds, as well as colonies of ants, frogs, and beetles, cover them. Fish trail these microbiomes, eating the insects that slough off their fragile edges.

"Bon!" Robert shouts.

He reels in his line and recasts to starboard. Before I can ask what's going on, the answer flies into the air. It's a school of *Pantodon buchholzi*, or flying river fish, hundreds of them leaping above the surface. Some tribes believe these fish perform at the behest of the river gods, acting as offstage dancers cued by spasms of love. According to the folklore, each leap celebrates a celestial orgasm.

"Cast your line," Robert orders. A devoted piscatorial warrior, he's eager for battle.

But I'm entranced by the eurythmics of belly-flopping fish, their bodies silvered mirrors coughed up by the river. Considering the number of frenzied leaps, the gods are proving themselves truly superhuman today.

Robert snatches my pole and casts with stunning accuracy, the hook landing inches ahead of the flying fish, which he says are feeding on minnows; large river perch should be chasing them as well.

"We want the perch!" Robert bellows.

A hornbill resounds somewhere in the emerald hills, and its raucous cry sets off an avalanche of sounds. Hundreds of jungle voices start shrieking and chattering. Robert works the lines while I try to identify each forest song.

"Voilà . . . I can smell them now."

I catch a watermelon scent wafting over the myriad other jungle smells.

"Oui. Parfum de melon . . . Delicious." Robert sniffs the air.

The flying fish head toward the middle of the river. Their leaps are subsiding; perhaps even the gods need a break. The smell of fresh watermelon intensifies. All the kingfishers are airborne and on the hunt, competing with gulls, pratincoles, terns, and skimmers.

"Yahoo!" Robert trumpets.

He has caught something. The rod flexes down to the water. Patiently Robert pays out some line, noting that he's "smarter than the fish," as if this might be a lingering question. Eventually, between guzzles of beer, he reels in a Nile perch, the largest species in the Serranidae family and a favorite among fishermen for its good flavor and the high price it fetches at market.

I decide to join the fray, but Robert lands three more fish before I manage to snag one. Mine must weigh twenty pounds. Robert leans over the rail, recoils, and grabs the wire cutters. Twang, he snips the leader.

"Hey . . ."

"I hope you know your dinosaurs better than your fish. That was a killer."

"Oh." I open a field guide and find a picture of the fish, *Malopterurus electricus.* The stumpy black swimmer with small fins and a blunt tail packs an electric charge strong enough to pierce thick leather gloves.

I'm watching Robert land another perch, when something grabs my line and nearly pulls the untended rod overboard. The fish doesn't put up much of a fight and is soon flopping on the deck. This one I recognize instantly. It's a *Protopterus*, an African lungfish, able to breathe on both land and water and, like Mokele-Mbembe, a carryover from the dinosaur age. They're not very tasty, so I toss it back. Robert tells me that in all his years fishing, he has never seen a lungfish in the Congo River.

"They're common in lakes and swamps, but not here."

I take the lungfish as a good sign that of all places on earth, the Congo is the most likely to harbor a living dinosaur. The climate in this region has changed little over millions of years; neither the Ice Age nor shifts in polar magnetism have had much effect. The jungle from here to Lake Télé is relatively unexplored, and an animal the size of a school bus could be roaming undetected. In fact, much of what once lived in Europe millions of years ago has lingered in equatorial Africa.

When the beer is gone, Robert weighs anchor and gooses the throttle. The engine roars angrily. Ring-ga-dindin-din. The hull pounds as the propeller whips the vessel up to nose-flattening speed. We fly down the Corridor, now stripped of features by our speed. Everything's a greenish blur. For one brief moment I feel as if I'm aboard a time machine hurtling through warped space, unable to determine whether we're racing into the future or into the past.

Robert steers a course between M'Bamou Island and the right bank, slowing the boat as we enter the channel. Long ago I read about a maurauding tribe of cannibals, the Yakas, who migrated from the north and terrorized the Kongo Kingdom in the seventeenth century. The Yakas set up their victory kitchens on M'Bamou; for a month they stoked cook fires that turned human prisoners into stew. The leader of the cannibals was called the Great Ghaga, and his army was unstoppable until the Portuguese appeared with guns and cannons. The story of the Yakas was related by Andrew Battell, an English freebooter and slaver they captured but decided not to eat. He eventually escaped and wrote a memoir that kept me up many nights as a child.

We leave two sandbars to port and enter a maze of small islands. As we round the bend leading to the fabled Yaka kitchen, I'm startled by the sight of dozens of powerboats pulled up on a sandy beach. Topless French and Congolese women wave at us from a volleyball court. Beachballs and blankets lie scattered about under large umbrellas bearing the names of French apéritifs. A group of men tending a charcoal grill shout at us. Robert holds up his catch for them to admire and says he'll be back as soon as he drops me off.

"No fish?" the window washers ask me back at the ferry landing.

"My friend caught plenty. One was this big." I stretch my hands out two feet.

"This is Clément and I'm Medard."

Medard is a head taller than Clément, and I tower over Medard. They profess to be the best window washers in Brazzaville.

"Yesterday we were at the president's house. We want to show you something." Medard points toward an overturned plastic bucket.

"Look," Clément urges.

Underneath the bucket is a host of butterflies: swallowtails, snouts, whites, judys, and a few charaxes.

"They are for you," the men chorus, proudly showing me how they caught the butterflies with their shirts.

Together we flip through a field guide and identify them one by one. The blood-red *Cymothoe sangaris* is voted the prettiest, and we cheer as it flies to safety in the kapok tree.

They're reluctant to accept my invitation to the Palm Club until I assure them that it will be my treat. They both have bicycles and insist that I ride one while they double up on the other. At the top of the hill, they start chiming the handlebar bell and singing.

"Luciole. Une tête de la luciole. Luciole, ohhhh, luciole, Monsieur Luciole. Luciole. Une tête de . . . ," they sing, pointing at my head, saying it shines like a lightning bug.

CHAPTER ◆ 7

M ONDAY. BACK TO THE ROUTINE. Two pots of coffee have fueled me to keep apace in the stream of workers funneling down Cabral Avenue. Most of the men wear spotless white shirts and pressed black pants, the women fluorescent print dresses or colorful busbuses. Of course, everyone carries an umbrella.

As usual, there's a bottleneck this morning near the post office, where an ancient silk cotton tree stands in the road, forcing motorists, bicycles, and pedestrians to squeeze into one lane. Remarkably, no horns are honked and no curses yelled. The tree has always been here, and people reach out to touch it as they pass.

In the animist culture of the Congo, trees are revered as the homes of spirits. By law, before an old tree on city property can be cut down, a witch doctor must be summoned to entice its spirit into taking up a new residence. This process can take months, even years to complete. One unresolved case dating back to 1963 pits a mighty baobab spirit against a team of road engineers. Nine witch doctors have tried to vanquish the spirit, but each has failed. The tree is known locally as "the wood that wouldn't." The Brazzaville Highway Department leaves such trees where they are and simply paints the trunks white.

▼

"Drivers must be alert. Cars must go slow," the supervisor of a work gang explains. "The tree was here first."

As other commuters rush by, I stand and watch a road crew laying asphalt, impressed by the respect they accord a *Schizolobium*, cousin to the more familiar cigar tree. The three men packing asphalt around it are careful not to rip the bark or damage the roots.

"The spirit must breathe," one worker says, upbraiding a colleague who has splashed tar on the bark.

The crew chief nods in assent.

Timber companies employ legions of witch doctors to placate both the displaced spirits and these traditionalists.

"Most of them are frauds," Fortunado told me one night at the Palm Club. "I know of a witch doctor who claimed he relocated the spirits of an entire forest in one day. Ha! Impossible! The older the tree, the more comfortable the spirit and the harder the job!"

"How do you know when a tree spirit has moved on?" I asked.

"Inside," he said, rapping his chest. "I can feel his presence and I can feel his absence."

◆

"Excusez-moi," a startled man apologizes later in the day, his knee still lodged in my side as I'm tying my shoelaces outside the Ministry of Forests.

"Ah, bonjour, Roger," I say, recognizing the museum curator I met last week at a Nigerian embassy party. He works at the Museum of Ethnography, better known as the Fetish Museum.

"Are you still interested in visiting the museum? I'm headed there now." He points to his car. Since the museum is open by appointment only, I accept the invitation.

We drive several miles to a wealthy neighborhood, park the car, and walk down a shady street, passing tidy peastone paths leading up to ornate front doors. On either side of the street are lovely cassia and frangipani trees planted in an alternating pattern, the tall cassias ripe with clusters of golden flowers and the petite frangipanis exuding their alluring fragrance. The wind gusts, sending bell-shaped cassia blossoms tumbling into the air.

"There's a party up there somewhere," Roger says of the wind. "The sky gods are playing music for a party of tree spirits." If rain starts falling, it will be a sign that the water gods have joined the party.

As we near the museum, Roger tells me that it was founded by Victor Malanda, a self-styled Christian prophet who railed against fetishism. Secretly bankrolled by missionaries, he bought up all the fetishes he could find, often sweetening the deal with free crosses and Bibles. People flocked to his house, happy to sell or trade their spent fetishes. "The Bibles made great tinder," Roger explains. "Not many people could read in those days."

A fetish, Robert continues, is not meant to be worshiped; it's merely a shell for the spirit, and nothing is too ugly, simple, or small for the task.

"A lock of hair or a toenail clipping tied to a string will sometimes do the trick."

Each fetish is consecrated to a specific task, its power limited only by the imagination, and once its mission is accomplished, the spirit vacates the container. Believers employ witch doctors for any number of reasons; revenge, however, tops the list. Litigation can take years in the backlogged Congolese justice system, so many people rely on fetishes and spells to exact justice.

"Voodoo and black magic are rooted here . . . Its power reaches all over the world," Roger says, reminding me that many rituals that we think of as indigenous to Haiti actually started here.

In a 1980 survey, more than half of the Congolese population declared themselves Christians, but ninety percent also said they visited a witch doctor at least twice a year. Roger himself receives Communion at Sunday mass, but he believes in animist spirits as well and calls on a witch doctor several times a month.

By law fetishism is banned. It's one of the few topics that the Catholic Church and the communist government agree on, but to little effect. In 1971 the government suspended the members of the Brazzaville soccer team when fetishes were found buried under the playing field. This led to the largest public demonstration since independence, and the government was forced to back off. The next soccer game was played on fresh sod, newly laid over hundreds of fetishes deposited by fans on behalf of the team.

The museum has the dank and musty smell of a mausoleum. "Bugs love it in here," Roger says, bemoaning the lack of air filters, humidity controls, and air conditioning. Since most of the collection is carved from wood, he has an ongoing battle with termites. "Unfortunately, they are winning."

He flips on a light switch, but nothing happens.

"Come stand over here . . . Feel it?"

A draft of chilly air raises goose bumps on my neck and arms. Although it's almost ninety-five degrees outside, its eerily cool where we're standing.

"Strange, eh?" He leaves me to ponder the source of the draft while he goes to the fuse box.

In the Himalayas, lamas sometimes divine the presence of spirits through changes in the air temperature and wind strength. Devils blow cold air, but benign spirits warm the air with their generous hearts. I wonder if the opposite might hold true in the tropics, where a cool breeze is more welcome.

There's a loud thump from the rear of the building.

"Are you all right?" I call into the darkness.

"Fine . . . just hit a display. No damage." Roger then lowers his voice to make amends to the fetish he bumped. This is no perfunctory apology but a lengthy supplication.

Recalling an old trick taught to me by a North African tribe, I pull out a coin and drop it on the floor. This act proclaims me a vassal of a nearby spirit and eliminates the need for it to demonstrate its power.

"Merde!" Roger fumes, flipping what sounds like a breaker switch. Click. "Merde." Click. "Merde . . ."

I reach into my bag for a flashlight and follow the clicking sounds until I find Roger, who takes the light and shines it on the fuse box.

"Wow," we both exclaim, looking at a rat's nest of wiring. The electrician who hooked up this panel must have been colorblind. Blue tails are spliced to red leads; black lines are crimped to yellow ones; green grounds run to hot posts; brown wires are soldered to white ones. The diagram on the panel door bears no relation to reality; even the polarity has been reversed on the top row of switches.

"Imbecile," Roger snarls.

"Or genius," I suggest, pointing out that the electrician has made himself indispensable. With 220 volts pulsing through the system, we decide not to fiddle with the wires.

Roger leads me into another room and shines the flashlight on the wall. A face jumps out at us. It's a ceremonial mask covered with a chalky whitewash. Mica has been brushed around the ears and under the cheeks and nose, highlighting the vivid countenance. Wispy black eyebrows arc quizzically across the forehead. Its beehive-shaped hairdo has been charred, smoothed, and glazed, and the finely carved lips appear to be whispering. I near the face for a better look and stare into the heavily lidded eyes.

"Pounou mask from the Niari Valley," Roger says. "We know very little about it, but the white chalk indicates ancestor worship."

Years ago it was a common practice among the lower Congo tribes to share in the estates of the dead. Whenever a chief or a great hunter died, his head was severed from the corpse and hung over a block of chalk, which absorbed the vital drippings. Worthy members of the tribe would then apply the chalk to their foreheads, believing that the wisdom and strength of the deceased would be transferred to them.

Roger flashes the light across a dizzying wall of fetishes: masks, statues, and carved animals. He highlights parts of each fetish to illustrate the similar shapes and patterns common to all of them, whether from the coast, hills, or jungle.

"They didn't have glue, so they carved everything out of one piece of wood," he says, pointing out that all the statues have straight, almost rectangular bodies, with small heads and no necks. The legs are unusually short in relation to the torso, and the sex of each fetish is plain to see. "And notice that none of the fetishes tell their stories . . . No allegories here."

The narrative of each fetish was the strict provenance of the village elders and witch doctors. Because no written form of Lingala or any native tongue existed until missionaries came in the mid-1800s, much of the old lore has been lost.

"Look at this one . . . from the Tsayes of the Lekouma region." Roger spotlights a fetish on the far side of the room. It's a disk-shaped bronze fringed with ornamental grasses and topped with an aureole of plumes. Blood-red eyes suggest a sinister spirit, but Roger doesn't feel that it was cast for an evil purpose: the feathers, in fact, are symbols of celebration.

The Kokongo tribes learned the secrets of metallurgy as early as the fourteenth century, the molten recipes trickling south from Arabs willing to trade secrets for slaves. The Congolese developed their own methods, such as converting hollowed-out termite hills into smelting ovens. It's doubtful, however, Roger says, that they would mix a batch of ore specifically for fetishes.

"After they finished making arrow tips, knives, and spear heads, they probably poured the excess into ground molds . . . Afterward the village witch doctor would sanctify and empower the object."

"Any Mokele-Mbembe fetishes?" I ask.

"Not that I know about, but it's possible . . . Ask the fetishes, one of them may respond."

No spirit answers my improvised call.

As we shuffle down a corridor lined with objects, I remember a disastrous high school trip to a glass museum and keep my elbows tucked tight to my body.

Roger stops, raises the light to a fetish in the corner, and blesses himself as he says, "There."

This fetish is painted red, black, and white, and although it's almost four feet tall, it looks as if it was pummeled down from a larger size. All its features appear scrunched, and its head is horribly misshapen. Half of its jaw is missing, and it is scarred by deep gouges. Two rows of chiseled teeth protrude from what's left its black lips. Blowgun darts serve as the hair, and a series of holes riddles the ears, neck, and shoulders. The grass skirt tied at its waist is belted with bones — human bones from the look of them.

"Don't!" Roger grabs my hand as I reach out to touch the skirt.

He blesses himself again.

"The teeth were pulled from the mouths of enemies. The holes are for trophies, you know, men's things."

The Yakas were not the only tribe to eat their prisoners of war. For centuries it was common practice for the triumphant to consume the defeated and thereby absorb their strength. The practice became less common after Europeans arrived and began buying prisoners for shipment to the west.

At night, when I catalogue the feathers, beetles, and butterflies I've nabbed during the day, I always scrounge through the bottom of my camera bag for the odd seed or leaf. Tonight, though, I prick my finger on something sharp. It's a tooth with a chiseled tip.

CHAPTER 8

C ONGRATULATIONS, I HEAR you got your permit," a member of the Leisure Board greets me at the Ministry of Sports, Leisure, and Tourism.

"Thanks," I reply warily, waiting for the punch line to yet another joke about bald dinosaur hunters, but this time he shakes my hand.

What's the source of this rumor? A typist says his friend has heard it from another friend who was told by a clerk at the Forestry Department. This is the sort of gossip to encourage; surely, one way to make something happen is to have people presume it has already happened. After all, rumors are the currency of the bureaucracy and increase in value each time they're traded.

"I'll send you a card from the jungle," I promise, dodging outside for the next bus heading toward the Ministry of Forests.

On the ride I think of Karl May, an early twentieth-century German travel writer, whose books consistently outsold the Bible. An expert manipulator of rumors, he hoodwinked a generation of readers with a series of fabricated adventures about his exploits in remote corners of the world. Cloistered in a Bremen warehouse, he set up his deception by writing postcards and paying sailors to mail them from exotic ports at prearranged intervals. Gullible newspaper columnists received the cards and dutifully reported his progress. All the while, without leaving the warehouse, May was composing his grand tales on a typewriter. At the end of a journey May would emerge, his adventures accepted as fact. When he was eventually found out, he blew his fortune defending his lies to an unsympathetic court.

The secretary at the minister's office greets me with a large smile.

"You came at just the right time . . . This typewriter is giving me trouble again."

He has heard absolutely nothing about my permit, and he doubts it could have been drafted without his knowledge. My head pounds with a sudden pain. The celebratory drink I've been anticipating will have to be a medicinal tonic instead.

But miraculously, a day later — forty days and nineteen hours after my first application for a permit — the minister calls me to his office.

"I hope the wait hasn't been too long," he says, breezing into the reception room where I'm sitting.

"No problem," I lie, trying to smooth out the wrinkles in my jacket. He's wearing a tailored silk suit and a crisp white shirt.

"Follow me, please."

As the secretary mentioned, the minister is not a man for small talk. Oil revenues are down this year, and the government is relying on his office to cover the shortfall. Sixty percent of the rain forest has just been opened for logging after it was reported that the Japanese would loan a large sum to the Congo in exchange for an increase in its timber quota. Somehow the minister must find a way to guarantee the increased production.

"So you want to go to the jungle and look for Mokele-Mbembe?"

"Yes, sir!"

"Well, good luck." He hands me a travel visa two pages long, single-spaced and written in French. Even the first few words of legalese are beyond my vocabulary. I pull out my pocket dictionary.

"Please close the door on your way out." The minister nods and returns to his work.

Two staff members are waiting for me in the reception room. A few details, I'm told, must be clarified. A pile of contracts is plopped on the table. The language is ponderous and severe; it will take me a full day to translate everything.

"Oh, no . . . You must do it now. Nothing leaves this office unless it's signed," says the older of the two men. He's wearing a Congolese red star on one lapel, a pin of Lenin on the other, and a tie tack embossed with Chairman Mao's chubby countenance. Gauging him the equivalent of a lawyer wearing both a belt and suspenders, I decide not to argue. His partner is wearing a Mao jacket, no doubt a leftover from the mid-sixties, when all Congolese workers were ordered to wear such outfits — an unpopular law that was rescinded within a year. At this point, I'll sign anything in exchange for the permit, and my pen dances across the bottom of several pages.

"What's this?" I hold up a document entitled "Escort Services."

"You will be assigned a man . . ."

I ask about Ambroise, knowing his heart is set on going; indeed, his home decorating plans depend on this assignment. However, they've never heard of Ambroise and don't care to hear about him.

"You go with our agent," they insist.

I sign the document.

The secretary returns with my new escort, a friendly-looking man about my age dressed in the simple green uniform of a forestry agent. Unlike Ambroise, he looks quite fit and has a quick smile. A field guide sticks out of his back pocket.

"Je m'appelle Innocent," he says.

▼

CHAPTER ◆ 9

W HY ALL THE BOOZE?" the American consul asks,
counting the cases of scotch and bourbon on the
tarmac.

"Law of the jungle," Innocent replies.

"Visas don't mean much in the north country," an air force
colonel explains.

The colonel, whose ancestral home is near Lake Télé, is
flying with us on the mail plane to Epena. Thanks to him, we
have learned of a few of the local customs, one of which
obliges outsiders to offer liquor and salt to every village chief-
tain along the way. The traditional gesture calls for a calabash
of palm wine and several handfuls of salt, but Innocent and I
have cleaned out a liquor store.

The mail plane is a twin-engine Cessna, once a six-seater
that now accommodates only four plus extra gas tanks. Jean,

our pilot, is decked out in a sky-blue uniform and a white ten-gallon hat.

"I spent two months at Mitchum Field in Texas getting certified to fly this here dogie," he says, trying to affect a Texas drawl.

Like his grandfather and father before him, Jean left France after his military service to seek adventure and fortune in Africa. In a few years, he says, he'll return to Paris, settle down, and raise a family. Until then he wants to fly as many miles as possible. Inclement weather has grounded him lately, though, and this morning's flight with the mail and the army payroll is two weeks late.

As Jean supervises the cargo loading, he takes special care with the cases of ammunition.

"Can't have loose shells rolling around, can we?" He uses duct tape to seal each carton before slipping them into a wing compartment.

We taxi to the end of the runway, and Jean sticks his hand out the window.

Kaboom! Kaboom! Two blasts cut through the engine noise. My fingers dig into the seat cushion.

"What was that?"

Jean points down the runway to a man holding a shotgun. "He's clearing out the birds." Before a plane lands or takes off, the airport warden rides his bicycle down the runway and fires his gun to scare off any birds or small animals. Once, Jean says, the man wasn't paying attention and peppered his tail with buckshot. "Now he uses blanks."

Kaboom! Another round is fired, scattering a reluctant flock of Senegal bustards. The warden signals all clear. Jean touches the Saint Christopher medal taped to the control panel, revs the engines, and releases the brakes. We gather speed and take off.

The plane loops around Brazzaville and flies low over Stanley Pool. The ferry docks on both shores are jammed with people; one boat is in mid-passage and the other blows a cloud of smoke as it chugs away from the dock. Off to port a munitions train rolls onto the docks at Pointe Hollandaise; to starboard a tug pulls a line of barges from Kinshasa, headed, it appears, for Pointe Hollandaise.

"That train doesn't exist," the colonel announces, gesturing toward the flatcars loaded with field guns and tanks.

"Angola bound?" I ask. The tanks look Russian built. The colonel remains silent. Is it possible that the United States and the Soviet Union share the same supply lines through Zaire?

"The train is a mirage," the colonel insists.

"Mobutu is getting cash from both sides?"

"Look, it's not there!"

"Right."

Epena is the administrative center of western Likouala Province, just fifty kilometers from Lake Télé. The colonel describes Epena as a town marking the boundary of the twentieth century.

"It's the last place with electricity for hundreds of kilometers. They even have televisions."

I suppose a television is as good a geographic marker for modern society as anything else; surely it's a better indicator than a church bell. I wonder how many channels they receive.

"When I was last there five years ago, they got 'Kojak'!"

Jean unfolds a chart that makes me uneasy. It's the same one I have: out of scale, poorly marked, and badly printed.

"We follow the rivers almost all the way," he tells me. "First the Congo and then the Ubangi and finally the Likouala aux Herbes, which goes right to Epena."

Below us the Congo River is like a brown snake slithering through a green nest. The verdure stretches beyond the horizon, the crowns of thousands of trees swaying as one. Tall grass flanks most of the river, suggesting the breadth of the floodplain, but a few trees hang over the banks, their limbs scratching the snake's back.

Jean keeps the plane low, never ascending above a thousand feet. He's a volunteer member of a conservation group studying the migratory patterns of hippos and jungle elephants.

"Look for anything big that moves."

Within the hour, Innocent sights a horse-sized bongo, several pairs of duikers, and a herd of sitatungas or bushbucks. The colonel sees a wide swath through the grass that Jean says is an elephant trail. He places an X on the map to mark the spot.

I'm little help to Jean's cause. My thoughts are locked on Mokele-Mbembe, my eyes scanning for the god-beast's cousins, the duckbills and boneheads that once prowled the area. I recall Professor Bowers's words to me in Cambridge: "Who knows what's out there?" It's safe to say that below me are more species of flora and fauna than exist in all of North America, but no one knows exactly how many. Up until the early 1970s, scientists estimated that there were approximately one million species of insects in the world; since then, research has raised the estimate to somewhere between thirty and forty million, and more than half live in tropical rain forests. Among the multitude of undiscovered or uncatalogued life forms, why shouldn't there be a family of dinosaurs?

As we near Liranga, a town across the river from Lake Tumba and near the mouth of the Ubangi, Jean sighs deeply. We've flown 180 miles without spotting a single elephant or hippo.

"Four years ago there was wildlife all along this route. Always a few hippos and sometimes dozens of elephants."

I remind him that it's almost noon, siesta time for the big animals. Hippos spend the hottest part of the day in the water, where they would be hard to spot from a plane, and elephants usually snooze in the shade.

"I hope you're right," Jean says, and updates us on the bleak statistics for their declining populations. If the trends continue, Jean says, both hippos and pachyderms will all be gone forty years into the next century.

For the past half-hour the river has been widening, and now it stretches eight miles across. The mountains have receded

and given way to the fabled Congo Basin, the alluvial plain that is the heart of the African continent. It extends beyond the horizon in all directions.

We fly close to Liranga, where a flotilla of boats lies offshore. Crafts of all sizes and shapes are here: canoes, speedboats, tugs, river freighters, and barges an acre in size. Jean dips down for a better look.

One anchored tug is lashed to a pod of three barges unlike any I've ever seen before. They appear to be floating sections of city blocks, three stories high, with bustling street scenes atop their corrugated roofs. Laundry snaps in the breeze; children herd goats; chickens hunt and peck; people ride bicycles, crossing from barge to barge on planks. As we approach the craft, I see that the verandas ringing each deck are actually crowded marketplaces. Scores of canoes are tied alongside the barges, nuzzling the mother ship like hungry offspring. The water off Liranga, I learn, is a principal meeting place for river traders, fishermen, hunters, and farmers.

"That's an entire city down there. Five thousand people or more . . . It's the floating capital of Central Africa." As a teenager the colonel visited these barges frequently, and he says it's not unusual to meet people aboard who have never lived on land. "You can buy anything down there . . . The gangways are one store after another. There are midwives and undertakers."

People come to barter fresh game, manioc, vegetables, salep, and fish for clothing, ammunition, and other manufactured goods. With the yearly inflation rate in Zaire exceeding

350 percent, people would rather have merchandise than cash.

There are bakeries and restaurants aboard the barges, as well as machine shops and other businesses. Occasionally a Zairese police boat will visit, and officers will try to round up anyone without a ticket or traveling papers; otherwise, shipboard life operates by its own laws. One long-term barge resident serves as mayor and arbitrator. If the mayor can't settle a dispute, then the tugboat captain has the final say.

A puff of smoke belches skyward from the tug's bowels. Jean swings the plane around for another look. Crewmen head to the bow of the tug and start working the windlass to raise the anchor. Apparently, things haven't changed much in the century since the first motorized craft chugged up the Congo. That boat, the *En Avant*, was built in Belgium and shipped piecemeal to the Pool. Like the *En Avant*, the tug and other big ships below us were all fabricated in foreign yards and the pieces crated for assembly above the rapids. Judging from all the timber stacked on the tug's fantail, it looks as if she's powered by the same kind of wood-fired steam engines that took Conrad upstream.

The tug blows its whistle, and as we circle the barges and watch, swarms of people begin clambering over the rails into their canoes, their arms loaded with merchandise. Others run around grabbing their children or gesture wildly with their hands, making their final offers to merchants.

As the tug pulls the barges upstream, a white-shirted crewman cuts loose any canoes still tied alongside. People start diving off the rail. One man is frantically waving from the roof. Jean tips the wings, and we head back on course up the river.

We pass over a sailboat, a lone triangular shape among ovals, cigars, and rectangles. The boat is on a reach, and it easily outdistances a pirogue with eight paddlers. This is the first sailboat I've seen on the Congo, though I've been told there's a yacht club near Boma, on the ocean side of the rapids.

Jean strays into Zaire's air space, agitating the colonel a bit. Jean wants to show me where the Congo becomes the Zaire, which I learn isn't an African word, but a Portuguese mispronounciation of its ancient name: Nzere, or the river that swallows all rivers. Jean gestures toward the Ubangi River off the port wing, and indeed, it looks as if it's being swallowed up by the Congo. Its mouth is impossible to locate among all the islands and sandbars scattered throughout the debouchure. As we pass over, I realize how easy it was for Stanley to mistake all these islands for an extension of the right bank. He never sighted the Ubangi during his various trips, and when natives later pointed to the area on maps and talked about the "Tékota," or the Great River, Stanley is said to have had them flogged for lying to him. He was positive that the Congo was the only great river of Central Africa, and he considered himself far too expert a navigator to miss something as big as the Tékota. Like the Royal Geographic Society, Stanley believed that the Uele and Bomu rivers, which rise near Lake Albert in Uganda, flowed north and fed the Niger River system. Stanley left Africa before Captain Marchand, the French explorer, proved that the Uele and Bomu eventually merge to form the mighty Ubangi. Even so, the course of the Ubangi wasn't accurately mapped until the Franco-Belgian Treaty of 1914, which established the river as an international frontier.

At the time, the Ubangi was best known for what an irreverent British publication dubbed "a local predilection for Frenchman stew." Parisians, too, were transfixed by reports describing cannibal attacks on French garrisons on the Ubangi. One French newspaper urged the army to dispatch troops "to discipline the heathens . . . and teach them proper table manners."

Thwack! Innocent slaps me below my left ear.

"Merde!" A sharp pain drills into my neck.

"Sorry, but it was ready to bite. Did it get you?" Innocent

picks something off my shoulder and holds it up for me to inspect. "Damn," I groan, spreading the legs of a squished spider. Its spinnerets are exceptionally long, and I don't need a field guide to recognize this mottled species of the hersilid family. As with a bee sting, the pain from the bite recedes quickly, but not the itching.

Jean speculates that the spider bite is an omen. "Maybe you've been cursed . . . Bad magic."

"Bah," I say dismissively, clutching the juju bag Fortunado assembled for me.

Ahead a silver-topped building reflects the sun like a signal mirror. Jean says it's the center of Longo village, the turning point for our westward leg. He buzzes the area, scattering chickens and goats. A woman shakes her fist at us.

"Ah, there he is." Jean points out a man waving a white towel. He's part of a team that monitors the planes carrying government payrolls.

This overland segment of the trip is dangerous, and Jean doesn't like flying it when the radio beacons aren't working, as they aren't today. He accelerates as we change course and head west-northwest, ever deeper into the rain forest. The rpm needles jump, the engines thunder, and a trickle of oil seeps out of the starboard engine housing. Every few minutes he wets his thumb to touch the Saint Christopher medal mounted on the instrument panel. "If we go down near a river," Jean says, "we'll be found, but the jungle will swallow every trace of us."

Thirty minutes later, a collective sigh of relief goes through the cockpit as we raise the Likouala aux Herbes River. The river is a crooked, muddy flow here, stumbling through the forest. Scattered along it are dozens of oxbows, stagnant land-locked sections of the old channel in various stages of eutrophication.

There are three ages in the life of a river, and right now

we're looking at a granddaddy, a river far beyond its prime. Youthful rivers are characterized by steep gradients, rapids, and swift currents. This old-timer moves at a snail's pace over relatively flat areas, having reached a state of equilibrium with the land; instead of downcutting or carving a bed, the water drifts lazily off onto the easiest path. A fish would have to swim three miles on this loopy river for each mile that a bird flew.

Jean busily jots figures on a clipboard. He triple-checks his calculations and taps the fuel gauges with the eraser of his pencil.

"Looks good," he announces. "There's enough gas for a short detour. Lake Télé, anyone?"

CHAPTER ◆ 10

I T'S 1 2:5 5 P.M., with the temperature and humidity matching in the high nineties. Up ahead, from ground zero to the
heavens, is a wall of vapor. Seconds later we're flying blind
through a dense fog, and a clammy dampness envelops everything in the cockpit.

"It clears up once we're halfway through the great swamp,"
Jean reassures us.

"Swamp?"

"Don't you know about the swamp around Lake Télé?"

I know little about the geography between Epena and the
lake. Only four expeditions have made it to Lake Télé, and
their reports, like Congolese maps, are colorful but poorly
detailed. To prepare for this trip I consulted a variety of experts on things tropical and prehistoric, yet now that I think
about it, none of them had ever been to the Congo.

Jean points to the plane's compass. Two years ago, he says, an international advisory instructed all pilots to steer clear of Lake Télé. A crew aboard a flight bound for the Central African Republic had recorded wild compass gyrations in the area, and a few months later an Air Congo crew experienced the same phenomenon.

I pull out my pocket compass, but it's not behaving unusually.

The fog thins out, revealing a hellish landscape: a jumble of black, stunted trees rooted in a pool of charcoal muck.

"I once went to the edge of the swamp, and I'll never go back," the colonel says. "Too much tsetse and malaria and snakes."

As if by magic, the green forest reappears.

"Thar she blows!" I exclaim, sighting the leviathan shape of Lake Télé breaching the emerald forest.

The elliptical body of water is dark and mirror smooth, about five miles long and four wide. Along its edges are numerous lagoons and coves, and acres of lily pads hug the eastern shore. The plane's shadow, which was clearly visible on the treetops, is swallowed by the murky water. I imagine Lake Télé as a giant vat of primordial matter unchanged since a meteor gouged out its bed millions of years ago. Tree branches dip low, then spring upward, suggesting monkeys on the run. Many of the trees ringing the lake appear to be cycads and tree ferns, among the most primitive flora in the world.

Jean circles and makes another pass. Along the northern shore, several cormorants perch with their wings stretched out to dry, bearing a striking resemblance to pterosaurs.

"Perfect," I muse out loud, anxious to descend. "Absolutely perfect."

CHAPTER II

L ooks good," Jean surmises, eyeing the lumpy clearing a half mile from Epena.

I swallow hard and tighten my seat belt. The airfield is less than a city block long and is surrounded by hundred-foot trees.

Jean flies over three times to get a fix on termite hills and craters. The larger ones could easily snap the landing gear. On the second pass, a man trots into view and yanks an orange windsock up a flagpole. It droops, but Jean pays it no heed; instead he studies a plastic bag tumbling down the airstrip.

"Southwest breeze. Seven, mmmm, call it six knots." Jean says to himself. "Let's see . . . I'll bring her in at an angle. Got to watch those two big termite hills . . . Correct course once we're past the trees and . . . ."

To one side of the clearing is the rusty carcass of an army helicopter, a tree rising through its roof, the rotors and windows gone. The colonel was in charge of the crash investigation.

"The pilot told me that the jungle just sucked away the air. Usually, it's an updraft."

"Not now, Colonel," Jean snaps, and touches the feet of Saint Christopher twice.

We touch down, bounce, touch down, bounce, touch down again, bounce, and finally stay on the ground, grinding to a halt in the shade of an ironwood tree. Jean exhales and taxis over to a dilapidated building with a bowed roof and walls covered with lianas. On its façade the greeting "Bienvenu" has been painted out with whitewash. Jean cuts the engine as four soldiers march out of the building and surround the plane. The payroll is weeks late, and they're eager to secure it. The postmaster follows, dressed in blue cap and jacket but no pants.

"Where are your pants?" the colonel demands.

The man snaps to attention and salutes. "At the river being washed, sir!"

The postmaster is all business, despite his attire. He refuses to sign for the mail pouch until he has thoroughly examined the bag and its seal. Satisfied that Jean hasn't abused government property, he secures the pouch to the rear bumper of his moped with five bungee cords. He nods to Jean and salutes the colonel.

"Work!" he announces before beeping the tinny horn and shouting out commands at imaginary obstructions. "Make way! Government business . . . Make way!"

As the soldiers carry off the strongbox, a member of the town council introduces himself and gestures to a path crowded with people. Apparently all town activities have been suspended because of our arrival.

"Everyone loves to watch the planes. Please go into the air and land again."

Jean declines, but the councilor persists: "Do it again. It has been a long time . . ."

It turns out that we're the first plane to land here in more than six weeks, and we may be the last for a while. The field requires three days of sunshine without rain to be usable, and that's a rare occurrence in Epena.

Jean can't be talked into another landing. I try to ease the councilor's pained look with a fifth of scotch, but the crowd surges forward, everyone reaching for a bottle.

Innocent says something in Lingala that quickly soothes them. A few pat me on the back.

"What did you tell them?"

"I promised them a big party, la grande fête. Tonight, my friend, you will be opening many bottles in honor of Marien Ngouabi."

Marien Ngouabi, the former Congolese president, was a northerner born into the Kouyou tribe, regional cousins of the local citizenry. His assassination in 1977 secured his place in contemporary mythology. In Brazzaville it's rare not to see his portrait conspicuously displayed in a store.

"Ngouabi is more than a hero in the provinces, he's a saint . . . Remember, he's the one who kicked out the Americans and closed your embassy."

I remind Innocent that it was Alphonse Massamba-Débat, not Ngouabi, who gave the Americans their traveling papers in 1965. A diplomat back in Brazzaville showed me the office where Consul-General Frank Carlucci camped behind barricades as an angry mob outside took potshots at the embassy.

"Don't tell that story around here," Innocent advises.

Jean notices a bank of dark clouds rolling over the western horizon, and he urges us to help refuel and unload the plane quickly so he can take off before the storm hits. I crawl into the tail section to man the hand-operated fuel pump as Innocent fills the wing tanks. The colonel issues orders to the cargo handlers with a well-practiced cadence. Jean checks the oil and conducts the preflight inspection.

It's sweltering inside the fuselage. Sweat is pouring off me, and I have to wrap my T-shirt around the pump handle to keep a grip.

Jean checks the thermometer taped next to Saint Christopher. "It's 118 degrees . . . Welcome to the rain forest."

Minutes later the pump is sucking air, and Jean helps me coil the hose. Quickly he opens a small leather bag and extracts a tiny wooden doll dressed in woven grasses, with two emerald sequins for eyes.

"For luck," he says, pressing the fetish into my palm. I open my juju bag to give him a charm in exchange, but he declines, saying that I'll need all the help I can get.

"Don't cut your nails when the moon is full . . . Say a prayer every time you hear an owl . . . Don't step on anyone's shadow . . . Keep one fetish under your pillow at night . . . Put your left shoe on first . . ."

The soldiers hustle everyone off the airstrip. Parents hoist children onto their shoulders. Two soldiers check to see that all dogs are restrained. The colonel says an unleashed dog almost caused a fatal crash at another airstrip last year. The village councilor gives Jean the thumbs-up signal, and the engines roar. The plane bounces down the field, clears the treetops with two feet to spare, and disappears.

Most of the people straggle back to town, but a sizable group surrounds the colonel. "My family," he explains, introducing Innocent and me to twenty-eight adults and sixteen children. He assigns the oldest boys to carry our gear, and they tote it off down the path. He then sits down for a moment on a dining room chair brought especially for him.

"It's a sign of respect," Innocent says softly.

Overhearing this, the colonel chuckles and corrects him. "They think I'm rich and want to butter me up before asking for loans . . . They even brought canoes."

Although Epena is only a half-mile away by foot, the river route is a two- to three-mile paddle ride. "But it's the way chiefs and kings always traveled," the colonel says.

After posing for several Polaroids, we walk to the end of the runway, near the river. At the head of our procession is the regal chair, carried high by the colonel's oldest brother. Their grandfather brought the chair home from Impfondo, where he traded animal skins for it. "Six kilos of skins for six kilos of chair."

We reach the edge of the Likouala aux Herbes, where three pirogues wait for us. Two of them are carved from kapok trees, but the third has been adzed from a blond, unfamiliar-looking wood.

"What is this pirogue made from?" I ask one of the colonel's cousins, who is struggling to push the boat off the shore.

"Wood, of course."

"Yes, but what kind of wood?"

"Tree wood."

"Hey, give us a hand," Innocent groans.

I grab the rail. As the pirogue slides down the bank, the colonel's cousin speaks up: "It's a kapok tree. We just finished it . . . In a few days it will look like the others."

The chair is placed in the middle of one canoe, its legs wedged against the topsides. The smallest wave makes the top-heavy pirogue roll a bit, but a crewman assures the colonel that it's safe. The colonel gamely steps aboard, and the chair immediately topples over the side. The would-be throne is retrieved and stowed forward.

A flock of piping hornbills streaks by as we climb aboard. Six of them hug the riverbank, their long-beaked shadows stretching across the water, leading the way to Epena. Two red-bellied paradise flycatchers flit nervously from tree to tree, repeating their silvery calls, "See-see, see-see," until we shove off.

"Yee-iip-pa!" the paddlers chorus as their blades dip into the water. The three canoes stagger forward until the paddlers find their rhythm, and we glide along smoothly, the keel slicing through the water, raising little or no bow wave. I ride in the middle craft, following the colonel's boat, several boat lengths in front of Innocent's. Each canoe accommodates twelve, including four paddlers and a steersman. The strong-backed paddlers exhale loudly with each stroke, and it's obvious that they've worked together for years. They pause at the same moment, letting the stern kick out around tight bends, and resume paddling as one. The steersman, standing on the outboard edge of the transom, makes minute course corrections with his push pole; his main activity, though, is keeping the pirogue on an even keel by thrusting his hips and shoulders one way or the other.

The colonel's niece sits in front of me, a toddler dozing on her lap and newborn twins nestled on her hips in artfully tied maroon sashes. The twins awake within seconds of each other and she asks me to hold the toddler while she nurses the babies.

"Régine, je vous présente Monsieur Ami. Monsieur Ami, je vous présente Régine," she whispers into the child's ear as she passes the sleeping beauty to me.

Without opening her eyes, Régine yawns and stretches, retreating into a deeper sleep with her tiny hands clasped to my shirt and her head snuggled against my chest. I, too, start to relax and surrender to the jungle.

The paddlers keep to the shade and work their oars effortlessly. They no longer grunt; the paddles have become extensions of their arms. No one aboard speaks, and all cigarettes have been extinguished. It seems our lush surroundings have engaged everyone in conversation, one that doesn't require words.

The water sweeps by, gurgling sweetly under the myriads of jungle voices. Simple melodies float out from somewhere in the forest; closer to shore, warblers sing counterpoint. Barbets loose one-note *schreeps*, and gray parrots whistle. Every once in a while a hornbill joins in.

This section of the Likouala aux Herbes is fifty yards wide, half in jungle shade and half in sun. The slow-moving current barely ripples the reflections of the clouds in the water. Off to port, baking in the sun, the riverbank rises only a foot above the water, its top edge notched with animal paths. Behind it a wide strip of tropical grasses sways in the breeze, tickling the foot of the tremendous forest wall behind.

Watching me stare out over the floodplain, one of the paddlers says softly, "In the wet season the grass is under water and the fishing is good."

The right bank climbs high above the canoes, its soft face riddled with burrows of various shapes and sizes, suggesting a host of tenants. The trees on the bank are two hundred feet tall and are covered in a riotous tangle of creepers and epiphytes. Some of the vines dangle like monstrous tentacles groping for sunshine, others spiral around their hosts, content in the shade, and still more reach out for their own kind. Each arbor crown is a hundred feet in diameter and studded with small animals, birds, and nests. Millions of insects, I suppose, populate every tree. More often than not, the flora and fauna living on a rain forest tree outweigh the tree itself.

The river whispers *psst-psst* each time a paddle breaks the surface. Wherever there's a hole in the canopy, the sunshine dances through the foliage below and dapples the water. In small pockets scooped out of the jungle wall, tender half-lights glaze a leaf or gloss the bearded edges of a liana. Within every boat length, jade turns to emerald, emerald gives way to shamrock, shamrock turns back to jade.

I dangle a hand over the rail and dip my fingers in the warm water, letting all lingering tensions float downstream. Slowly I feel the river and its surroundings draw the poisons out of me, accomplishing what Fortunado, the witch doctor, tried unsuccessfully to do with potions and incantations.

A shoal of swallowtail butterflies rushes out from an acanthus bush. A few are attracted to the cool, damp interior of the canoe, and one lands on the rail next to me. Careful not to wake Régine, I reach out to pinch its thorax. Its distinctive green median marks it as a *Graphium gundenusi*. Certain Buddhist sects regard butterflies as chosen creatures sent to inspire and enlighten the human condition. They believe that Lepidoptera are often entrusted with messages from gods and spirits, but when I hold the butterfly to my ear, I discern only the soft flutter of wings struggling to be free. My fingers curl open, and the swallowtail vanishes into the sunshine.

We round a big bend in the river and see a small fleet of pirogues along the shore. "Epena," one paddler calls out. With home in view, the rowers pick up the pace and resume grunting.

The noise wakes Régine, and she looks up into my unfamiliar white face. "Wahhhhh," she bawls, tears streaming down her cheeks. My attempts to soothe her fail miserably. Her father, one of the paddlers aboard Innocent's boat, takes charge as we land. He can't be any older than twenty-five, so I'm surprised when he points out his six other children.

I follow the others along a mud path snaking up the riverbank. After years of anticipation, I'm about to step into an authentic village carved out of the rain forest. My pockets bulge with small gifts to hand out; from fishing hooks and small knives to pencils and packs of bubblegum cards featuring an American rock star.

"Epena. Bienvenu," the colonel says as we reach the top of the bank.

"Merci," I say, staring across an expanse of freshly mowed lawn. A gardener is operating a noisy weed-whacker around the base of a sago palm tree. Tidy houses fringe the far side of the lawn.

"This way," the colonel says, ushering me and Innocent into a manicured courtyard where cement statues of elves and frogs are surrounded by ornamental plants. Even by American suburban standards, the whitewashed brick house is large, and from somewhere inside, a tape player thumps out a heavy metal riff. I think it's Ozzie Osborne.

"Make yourself comfortable. Take a look around," the colonel says, excusing himself to visit his sister in the house.

Wanting to walk a bit, Innocent and I head up the nearest footpath and come to another open field; this one, though, is mostly dirt. Goats and chickens are wandering about, and children are playing soccer. Off to one side of the field is a junked Land Rover, its interior stripped. There's no sign of a road, and Innocent wonders how the vehicle got here. For centuries the main route to Epena has been the river.

"Welcome," says a man approaching us. His name is Guillaume, and he quickly offers his services as a guide. He wears a white shirt, black pants, and laceless black oxfords. Around his neck is the largest juju bag I've ever seen.

"It arrived on a barge one day," he says, pointing to the Land Rover. "Brazzaville issued a vehicle to every police district without checking a map. The commandant took everyone for rides around the field until it ran out of gas."

Guillaume invites us on a short tour of the town, and we follow him along dusty paths flanked by shrubbery and simple brick houses with galvanized roofs and gutters feeding into water barrels.

"My neighborhood," Guillaume announces proudly as we turn down a shady lane.

In ten short minutes, thirty years of daydreaming have been washed away. This part of Epena could pass for my parents' retirement community near Palm Beach. Hedge clippers and rakes are propped under the eaves of almost every house, the yards trimmed and pruned with care. The only stick houses are those being built by children with authentic Lincoln Log sets.

Innocent meanders over to a herd of goats penned in by a remarkable fence assembled from helicopter rotors, sticks, wire, and parts of the Land Rover. Guillaume shows me his garden, with flowers neatly laid out in geometric patterns, a circle here, a triangle there, its formality in stark contrast to the disorder of the jungle. I ask if his plants have medicinal or ritual uses. I once lived with a Berber tribe that grew roses in their desert compound, and although it was a twelve-mile ride to the well, the roses were essential to certain rituals.

"No, nothing like that," Guillaume says. "The designs are from an important book on gardens. This is a class project based on the work of Monsieur René Descartes. Do you know of him?"

"Je pense, ah . . ."

"Donc je suis," Guillaume coaches.

Guillaume, it turns out, teaches a high school course called "Great Thinkers of the World." Naturally, they're all French males. I suddenly realize that I must quickly derail him or we will be recapitulating several hundred years of Parisian café rhetoric. I ask him where to buy soap.

"What brand?"

We round up Innocent and stroll down a path lined with coral trees, the first I've seen in bloom. Innocent picks up one of the large, fleshy fruits that have fallen to the ground. Their sap is caustic, I warn him, and he drops it before his skin blisters. Several New World species of coral have leaves that can be eaten and flowers that are considered delicacies, but this particular species is cultivated for its poisonous properties. Fishermen grind the seeds of *Jatropha multifida* into a powder and sprinkle it on the water, stunning any fish in the area.

Guillaume veers off the path toward a saltbush tree, where a pile of roots has been stacked to dry. "Here, try this." Guillaume hands us each a piece of root.

Innocent works the root around in his mouth like a tooth-brush. The sap stimulates the gums, and the root fibers bristle into an effective brush.

We make our way to one of the few wooden buildings in town, a giant lean-to with rough-hewn boards on three sides, a tin roof, and an open front. A glass display case runs the entire length of the store. The owner is hunched over a Donald Duck comic book.

The shop is called Jamie's, but the owner's name is Idrissa.

"So many people are named Jamie that I thought it would be a good name for my store," he explains.

Idrissa isn't from Epena. He belongs to the mixed-blood mercantile class that operates similar establishments from here to Brazzaville. The colonial French trading companies usually manned their outposts with Senegalese, who often ended up marrying local women. After the French left, the tradition of Senegalese store owners and managers continued. His father is from Dakar, and his mother's family is from Mossaka, on the Congo River.

"Look at these beautiful knives. Genuine steel," he says, showing me a set of low-quality Chinese blades that carry Tiffany prices. The shop is stocked with a large assortment of items, from Sony Walkmans to paper clips. There are rows of dry goods, beans and cereals of all types, cake mixes, tins of pâté, several brands of instant potatoes, and various canned vegetables. Next to an arrangement of biscuits are cartons of fishing hooks, all of a better quality than those in my pocket. More tinned goods fill two long shelves; batteries are piled in tiers that reach the ceiling; hanging pots and pans clang in the breeze; socks and underwear are folded in boxes wrapped in cellophane. One advertisement over a perfume display reminds us, "We all want the smell of love." Directly behind Idrissa, in the men's toiletries section, are numerous brands of talc, colognes, deodorants, condoms, old French *Playboy* magazines, and six kinds of soap. Idrissa grabs a bar of Palmolive for me and plops it down next to his cash register, a wooden bowl.

"Look at this," Innocent exclaims, pointing at a poster advertising Michael Jackson's "Bad" album.

"The priest gave it to me," Idrissa says.

It turns out that some counterfeit merchandise seized in America several months ago was donated to Catholic Charities, which forwarded the goods to its regional office in West Africa. Several crates eventually made the trip upriver to Epena.

"Want to buy the poster? T-shirt? Pins? . . . Tapes? . . . ," Idrissa singsongs.

"I'll trade you two of these for the soap, okay?" I pull out two packs of cards, each containing a stick of gum and eight pictures of Michael Jackson.

He opens a foot locker brimming with the same cards.

I offer the pencils, fishing hooks, and small knives, but he shakes his head and says, "Cash or no soap."

CHAPTER ◆ 12

I AWAKEN THE NEXT MORNING with a nasty hangover,
remembering only that we toasted Marien Ngouabi end-
lessly; beyond that, my recollection of the party is as fuzzy as
the predawn light. Innocent is snoring next to me on the bed,
but I don't know where we are or how we got here. My clothes
reek of whiskey, and there's a horrid taste in my mouth, as if
I've licked several ashtrays clean. I force down five aspirins
and try to concentrate.

Our hosts, I discover, are sleeping on the other side of a
wattle partition. My gear is here, and everything appears to be
in order. There's a ceramic bowl near Innocent's pillow, but
I'm unsure whether it's a peepot or a water urn. Directly
overhead, three wasp nests cling to the main rafter; two appear
abandoned, but the third is definitely inhabited, and its residents buzz me periodically. The room is about ten feet square

and furnished only with the chunk of foam that serves as our mattress. Against the far wall is a doorway covered by a thatch panel.

I step outside to orient myself. Nothing looks familiar. A half-dozen footpaths radiate out from the house, so I opt for the one that seems to lead to a rising plume of smoke, hoping it's coming from the stove at the village café.

Along both sides of the path are rows of planted sago palms, looking like giant swizzle sticks from a Polynesian restaurant. Each of them has one or two gourds hanging from taps to collect the rich palm sap, which is fermented into a potent wine, which I don't want to think about right now.

Set back from the path, nearly hidden behind a stout hedge of flame vines, is a house that looks identical to the one I just left, making me wonder if I've walked in a circle. Looking closer, I can see it's a different building, however. Epena houses may share the same set of blueprints, but the residents embellish them with personal touches such as hand-painted shutters and window boxes. As I pass the grammar school, a low, rambling building with eight doors, a flock of paradise flycatchers on the playground stop preening their red, yellow, and green feathers, and we all exchange blinking stares.

"See-see-se-ah-seez," I call, hoping it's not too early for small talk.

The birds scramble skyward without a chirp. Their tail feathers, much prized for headdresses, stream out behind them. I stagger after the flock, my bleary eyes trying to focus on the plumes that only chiefs and great hunters may wear.

About seventy-five yards from the school the path dead-ends at a fifteen-story barricade of green. This morning, with a soft breeze stirring the foliage, the jungle wall looks like an enormous woven quilt hanging down from the sky. A corridor of scorched earth corrals its hem. Once a week, Guillaume told us, fires are set along the village perimeter to check the jungle growth; otherwise it would reclaim the town in a matter of months. From somewhere behind the wall a piping hornbill issues a raucous call.

"Baaaaahrooom!" I bay in return.

The jungle reports back with an orchestra of sounds, a legion of notes that meld in a pleasing way, quite different from the noises of the river. I recognize woodpeckers, babblers, honey-tongued warblers, coucals singing as one, finches, and gray parrots whistling up and down the scale.

As the sun begins to rise, nearly all of the wildlife community is stirring. The nocturnal feeders are hurrying through their last rounds; the daylight shift is awake and on the prowl, one eye out for food, the other searching for love.

The thought of food draws me back to the caffeine trail. As I had hoped, the fire has been stoked by the owner of the café. The postmaster, his only other customer, is sitting on his moped near one of the outdoor tables. He dismounts and asks me if the colonel is coming. I explain that we slept in different houses, but considering how late we celebrated, it's doubtful the colonel will appear any time soon.

"Good," the postmaster says, relieved. "I wouldn't want him to see me this way again." He points to his pants hanging from a date palm, drying in the heat of the cookfire. "They are clean, but still wet from yesterday's washing."

Other than his pants, he's dressed for work: pencils fill his shirt pocket, and various rubber stamps weigh down his regulation blue jacket; paper clips and rubber bands are wedged inside his hatband.

"Is there a plane due today?" I inquire.

"No, no . . . Maybe next week," he says, checking a pocket calendar. "It all depends on the rain." He glances skyward and adds, "That's a wet sky."

The café owner pokes his head through the doorway, and I order a large coffee.

"The mail should be here in an hour or two. There's so much to do," the postmaster sighs.

"Mail today?"

"Never-ending." A beleaguered look crosses his face. He bums a cigarette, lights it, and lets the smoke waft up and into his wide, pocked nose. He leans forward and says, "Mail is tricky business."

It turns out that the plane is only one of several courier systems. Once a day Pygmy porters carry mail pouches overland from Impfondo, the provincial capital, situated on the Ubangi about fifty miles to the east; other mail comes and goes aboard pirogues at unpredictable intervals. The twenty villages in the Epena postal district cover an area approximately the size of Holland.

The coffee arrives in a plastic mug with the words "I Love Christ" printed on it; in smaller lettering is "Compliments of the United Baptist Ministries." No matter, the coffee tastes delicious. When I compliment the café owner, he offers to show me the coffee bushes he cultivates behind his house. We make a date for later in the day, and I order another large cup of the home-brew.

"Do you know how many letters come and go from this station?" the postmaster asks, after checking his still damp pants.

"Many, I'm sure."

"Right. Dozens a day. I'm the best, but, monsieur, I am only one man, and they expect me to do the work of an army. I don't like to complain, but . . ."

His list of grievances threatens to go on for hours. "Did you enjoy the party last night?" I interject.

"Yes, thank you . . . Ngouabi was a great man. He was a northerner like us, you know. Believe me, southern tribes are not to be trusted." He launches into a tirade aimed at the Laris, Fangs, and Batekes; ironically, Ngouabi's life wish was to end this type of intertribal bickering.

The postmaster pauses to catch his breath and bum another cigarette. "They say you are leaving for Boha to look for Mokele-Mbembe."

"Yes, I am. Have you ever seen the beast?"

"I heard a great noise once years ago, upstream about fifteen kilometers. Sounded like thunder, but the sun was out. It had to be Mokele-Mbembe."

"Did you chase after it?"

"I am not a fool, monsieur. I ran the other way. You will understand if you stay here long enough. The forest is home to many, many spirits. Some are evil." His voice trails off as a raindrop splatters on the ground. "Au revoir, monsieur," he says, grabbing his pants and stuffing them under his jacket. He hops aboard the moped, tips his hat, and speeds off, beeping as he passes the kitchen door.

In minutes the sky changes from soft gray to greasy black. The wind kicks up, jostling the trees, and several miles away the clouds begin to grumble. The rain comes in giant drops.

Innocent is still sleeping when I race back into the house. We have unexpected company: a stray dog has come in through the doorway I forgot to cover. Considering the weather, I decide not to throw it outside; besides, he's better company than the snoring Innocent. He's a typical forest breed, with long legs, large muzzle, and short foxlike ears; his yellowish fur is caked with dirt. Jungle dogs are bred and trained not to bark; silence is the rule when hunting in the jungle, and each canine is expected to earn its living as a tracker. The tail and eyes do all its talking.

The skies open. Buckets of water cascade down the corrugated tin roof, thin streams leaking through the nail holes. As the downpour grows heavier, the rain striking the tin sounds like thousands of bouncing Ping-Pong balls.

"Hey, cut it out, please," Innocent groans as the noise increases.

"It's the rain."

"Oh . . . You're up and dressed. Good for you," he mumbles, falling back to sleep.

The dog thrusts his head into my lap as I sit on a bag near the doorway. Together we share what's left of a chocolate bar and watch the small puddles outside flow together to form a miniature lake. A fig leaf floats by with three ants and a beetle aboard. They patrol the edges, feelers out, searching for solid ground. The leaf spins around the corner, out of sight, into the high seas.

The equator is only seventy miles to the south, and the Atlantic lies five hundred miles to the west, which places Epena close to the true heart of Africa and absolutely in the center of the second largest rain forest in the world. The forest stretches for 1,500 miles from Cameroon to the Mountains of the Moon in Uganda; only the Amazon forest is larger. In an average year, Epena receives 80 inches of rainfall and once, in 1921, the skies dumped 112 inches. Even though the temperature remains constant throughout the year, Innocent told me that people still divide the year into four seasons: greater wet, lesser wet, greater dry, and lesser dry. Right now, in the last week of March, we're at the end of the driest part of the year.

The rain finally stops around ten o'clock, allowing the still groggy Innocent and me to search out the district military commandant. We need to have our visas stamped before we can depart for Boha, the closest village to Télé. Neither Innocent nor I can remember whether we met the commandant at the Ngouabi bash.

"Wonderful party . . . I enjoyed talking to you both last night," the commandant says. "I forgot to tell you that I've met several famous Americans. It was a reception for Mr. Eldridge Cleaver back in 19 . . . hmm, 19 . . . ?"

"1971," I offer, recalling the year Cleaver and other prominent members of the Peace and Freedom Party visited the Congo as guests of the state.

"Exactly, 1971. Do you know Mr. Cleaver?"

"By reputation only, sir," I reply, not wanting to break the news that the former radical ran for the U.S. Senate on the Republican ticket. As a born-again Christian, Cleaver now quotes Ronald Reagan and the Bible in the same sentence.

Both Innocent and I nod agreeably while the commandant relates stories "about the old days . . . when we were fighting the old order . . . when issues were black and white." Eventually he stamps our visas.

"There is one problem," he says, rising from his chair to wrap an arm around me in an avuncular fashion. "There's no petrol . . . no gas for the ferryboat, no gas for the generator."

By paddle, it's a twelve- to fifteen-hour boat trip to Boha, and since the arrival of outboard motors, no one will undertake the task. He describes the overland route between here and Boha as an "impossible, snake-infested" trek through miasmal swampland.

"You can go that way if you want . . . I'll write up something for you to sign, just so Brazzaville knows that you were warned."

We're left with two choices. We can either wait for the next pirogue from Boha and go back with the crew (there's no telling when that will be: it could be today or ten days from now), or we can hire Pygmy porters to fetch gas from Impfondo. It's a two- or three-day round trip, depending on the weather.

"Where can we find a porter?"

"Don't worry," the commandant says, his words somehow provoking the opposite response. He flicks a light switch. "The electricity has been off for weeks . . . It would be a shame to send porters all the way to Impfondo for a few liters of gasoline when the town generator has no fuel. Perhaps you will . . ."

I hand over enough money to hire three porters to tote

twenty-five gallons of gasoline, ten for the ferryboat and the rest for the generator.

Later in the afternoon, as we walk back from our tour of the café owner's garden, Innocent discovers that the porters maintain a cache of fuel nearby in the jungle. They've already delivered the town's fifteen gallons of gasoline, but our supply will not arrive for two more days. Now I better understand why the café owner said, "Everyone is happy to see new faces in town."

We run into Guillaume on his way home from school. He tells me that Marie, the village mystic, might know something about Mokele-Mbembe. We set off toward her hut on the far side of town.

"Watch it!" Guillaume warns, pulling Innocent to the side of the path. He was about to step on several eggshells lying at the base of a termite hill.

Once we leave the womb, we are unprotected and need the help of the gods to survive, Guillaume says. The eggshells symbolize man's birth and vulnerability; people often add them to their offerings of fruit to the gods.

Up ahead is a rickety structure built of sticks and dried mud, roofed with freshly picked palm fronds and plantain leaves. An old woman with hunched shoulders peers out from the tiny doorway and waves us into her cramped house. Marie's nose is rather flat and her skin has a reddish hue, indicating Pygmy blood. She stares at a pot on the kerosene stove, not looking up; as she meditates, I look around the hut.

On the shelves running around the walls are statues of Saint Anthony; there must be a hundred of them. In most he is holding a black baby Jesus. I had heard about the Antonian cult in Brazzaville, but I was unable to find a priestess of this outlawed sect, denounced by witch doctors, Catholic priests, and government officials alike. The cult was founded in the early 1700s by Kimpa Vita, a woman who claimed to have died and been resurrected by Saint Anthony. Among her miraculous powers was the ability to straighten bent trees. Kimpa Vita preached about a heaven full of black saints and a supreme black god. When she denounced the institution of slavery and demanded that the white man be thrown out of Africa, colonial officials burned her at the stake. Fearful that her bones would be used as relics, they burned her twice, until there was nothing left but ashes of ashes. Her followers express their devotion with statues of Saint Anthony.

Marie clicks off the stove and looks up at us. Her sunken eyes are abnormally large, and deep furrows run across her brow and cheeks. She wears a loose-fitting print dress and no jewelry, though there's a bit of twine tied around her neck. Her head is shaved, normally a sign of mourning.

She speaks softly, and Innocent leans forward to hear as they talk for several minutes.

"I've told her that we've come in search of Mokele-Mbembe. She wants to see your hand."

I put out my left hand. She grimaces and shakes her head.

"The right hand is the male hand. Left is for women," Innocent tells me.

She runs her fingers across my palm, applying pressure as she traces my lifeline.

"She wants you to think of Mokele-Mbembe and look into her eyes. She will see what you see."

Marie presses an ivory statue of Saint Anthony into my palm and folds my fingers over it. I begin to think of Mokele-Mbembe, black as night on the shore of Lake Télé, muscles rippling under its dark skin. When the beast turns its head, a lone tooth glints in the night.

"Bon!" Marie exclaims. She talks hurriedly in broken murmurs, injecting passages that sound like incantations. She sighs loudly, falls silent, and relights the stove.

"Well?" I ask.

"We must take a Toni with us if we want to see him," Innocent explains.

"Toni?"

"One of the Saint Anthony statues. A special one."

She holds out a well-carved antique ivory Toni. "Only forty dollars," she says. Innocent takes the Toni as I hand the bills to the priestess.

"Au revoir," Marie bids, and returns to stirring her pot.

Further questions about Mokele-Mbembe are met with silence. "Au revoir," she says again, sprinkling white powder into her pot.

"Magic potion?" I ask.

"No, the soup needs salt."

Guillaume rips into me once we're beyond earshot of Marie. He says Marie is old and sometimes forgets things, and I've taken advantage of her by buying one of the precious Tonis, part of a set that should never be broken up. The entire village relies on them to ward off devils, sickness, and infertility. Unlike fetishes, which may be used only once, Saint Anthony statues accrue power over time and can be used for an endless variety of purposes. Taking the statue is a sacrilege.

Innocent hands him the statue. There will be no refund, I'm told, other than what the gods decide to dole out. The collection of statues is restored, my wallet left thinner.

CHAPTER ◆ 13

THE VILLAGE LIGHTS sputter to life at eight on the dot. Minutes later the night air fills with soft chattering as people emerge from their houses and make their way toward the center of town. Innocent and I join the thirty people seated outside staring at a snowy television screen. Several other sets cackle in the background, but we stay put after a young boy grabs hold of the TV antenna, and an image of a sort flashes on the one channel. "Turn it slowly," someone tells the boy.

"Voilà!" people shout as the snow clears.

A grainy image of a man wearing a gorilla costume appears. He's beating his chest and growling something unintelligible. The screen goes black for a second, and then a man wearing a loincloth and belt studded with shrunken heads fills the screen. Twisted into his matted hair are chopsticks and more shrunken heads.

"Chasseur de têtes," Innocent says.

The camera pulls back to reveal a wrestling arena filled with thousands of shrieking fans. The ringside announcer delivers an extravagant introduction for the Gorilla of Zaire and the Headhunter. Tonight's match is for the heavyweight championship of Central Africa. The referee pulls the two wrestlers into the center of the ring, where instead of shaking hands, they immediately exchange blows and toss the referee to the mat. The fans around me leap up, cheering and whistling. The wrestlers strip off their warmup suits, and the featured "Battle Between Man and Beast" commences.

The Epena crowd is evenly split at first, but by the third round, when the Gorilla begins to tire, missing Atomic knee drops and flubbing Big Bang Missile kicks, everyone starts rooting for the Headhunter. The match ends in round five when the Headhunter hurls the Gorilla of Zaire into the second tier, apparently impaling him on a fold-up metal chair.

In place of a commercial, the program breaks for a five-minute message from President Mobutu, reminding viewers how hard the government is working to build a better Zaire. The Epena crowd isn't impressed and starts chanting for the next match as the screen scrolls images of President Mobutu visiting construction projects, factories, and hospital wards. Wrestling is Mobutu's passion, and thirty percent of TV Zaire programming is dedicated to his favorite sport. I've been told that diplomats regularly check the wrestling card before scheduling an appointment.

The action returns to ringside with a match between midget tag teams. I decide to go for a walk.

Moonrise is late tonight, and the dark sky is spangled with stars. This close to the equator both northern and southern constellations can be seen. Polaris is barely visible at the extreme edge of the northern heavens, while the tip of the Octant peeks over the brink of the southern sky; the Twins are about to disappear, and the Archer is creeping into view.

"Bonsoir, monsieur. Do you know the stars?" a female voice asks from somewhere behind me.

"A little," I answer, turning to see a gown floating toward me, its voluminous sleeves billowing in the soft breeze. The outline of a woman emerges. Her step seems unnaturally light, and I feel my pulse quicken as she approaches.

"What's that star?" She points to the southern sky. "The bright one, near those other four."

I try to focus on the heavens and not on her alluring scent of coconut and camphor.

"Up there, the bright star. Can you see it?"

Her slender forefinger is pointing to the Ship, a group of four constellations defining what the Ancient Greeks fancied as the final anchorage of the *Argo*.

"That's Canopus," I tell her, explaining that it's the second-brightest star in the sky, maybe two thousand times brighter than our sun.

"My mother said that is where my father's spirit is. She says he was too good for this earth."

I offer her a cigarette, hoping to see her face by the glow of a match; unfortunately, she doesn't smoke. We stand silently gazing up.

"I must tell my mother that he is two thousand times brighter than the sun. It will make her happy. Merci beaucoup, monsieur. Bonsoir." She turns and walks away, her dress streaming out again like a cloud.

I'm still lingering at the same spot at ten o'clock, when the wrestling matches end and the electricity is shut off. Children and parents shuffle toward home, and the singles begin their nightly promenade, or *mêlé masse*. The women walk in twos or threes, the men in packs of five or six, the groups exchanging shy, sly smiles as they pass.

"There he is. I can see his head," says a familiar voice.

I turn and see Innocent walking toward me with three men I don't know.

Innocent introduces me to Marc, Gaspar, and Alain. "They're musicians. They've invited us to a jam session."

"What kind of music?" I ask.

"Drums . . . the big sound," Marc replies, adding that he's the leader of the band.

"There's no one better than us," Gaspar boasts.

This is quite a statement, considering that Epena may be the percussion center of the world. The villages of Tom-Tom, Bongo, and Conga are all within paddling distance.

We walk toward the manioc fields and duck under an open structure with a thatched roof. Gaspar lights a kerosene lantern hanging dangerously close to the eaves. Marc snaps off a tarp covering the instruments: three tom-toms, several sets of bongos, two fifty-five-gallon barrels, and a seven-foot section of hollowed tree trunk with a slot cut in it.

Gaspar cradles a tom-tom while Alain props up one of the metal barrels. It's perforated with holes and shingled with rust. "You want old wood for your bongos and old steel for your drums. The rust adds to the sound . . . softens it," Alain explains.

Marc, who plays the large tree trunk, is the official drummer of Epena. "I send messages and interpret the ones that come in . . . Mostly, I play for entertainment. People love to hear the drums."

He makes a living by performing at weddings and traditional ceremonies, which, sadly, are less and less frequent here. Some of the smaller villages deeper in the jungle, though, maintain many of the old rituals. In Bontongo, for instance, there's a daylong celebration whenever a girl reaches puberty or a baby is born; twice a year there is a men's festival celebrating the birthdays of boys turning seven.

Alain and Gaspar work by day as fishermen, but drums are their passion.

"The drums are magic. They can make problems disappear," Marc says, and places a kiss on the big drum.

For centuries drums were the only means of communicating over long distances here. A finely tuned network of drummers maintained constant vigil, ready to relay messages anywhere in the Bantu universe. The drums rapped out messages in a common code that most tribes understood; it was the only way a Fang could talk to a Ubangi without an interpreter.

The first wireless was brought to Epena by Christian missionaries, but the local people were seldom allowed to send or receive messages. One priest required them to answer catechism questions before listening to radio news or music broadcasts. It wasn't until the 1960s that the air waves were freed in this part of the Congo, and telephones are still not in use.

The weather, more than anything else, affects the speed and clarity of drum transmissions. A cloudy day is best, as the low ceiling captures the sound and bounces it back to the ground. Rainy days are the worst: the drums must compete with the water noise and penetrate the sodden air. I ask how long it takes to send a message to Brazzaville.

"Four years ago I sent out a birthday greeting, and my friend got the message in three hours," Marc recalls, adding that any record would have been set years before he was born. In the old days the drums were used to warn of approaching slavers, French troops, and enemy tribes.

There's not a cloud in the sky tonight, so there's little chance that anyone in Impfondo will be able to hear the Epena drum, but if we're lucky, Marc might raise Boha to the west and Molembé to the east.

"Let's see who's out there," Marc says, rolling up his sleeves.

We step back as he closes his eyes and starts to shake his arms like a swimmer on the starting block. Suddenly the air whooshes past me, each whack of the drum supercharging the molecules around us. Dust and bits of thatch sift down on us from the rooftop. My body starts to vibrate to the tempo;

muscles loosen and bones start knocking. I feel like a freshly plucked bass string.

Boom-boma-rahbooom-boom-bam-boom-boma-rahboom-boombam . . .

Alain tells me that Marc is tapping out the standard salutation. Anyone in the area will recognize the distinct rhythm of Epena — the village call letters, so to speak. While we wait for responses, I'm appointed the timekeeper; the others will identify the replies as they come in.

"Bolé," Marc shouts, left hand cupping his ear.

"One minute and forty-eight seconds," I announce.

"Djéké," Alain notes, as another drum voice thunders.

"Ah, there's Boha. It's a little weak, but that's their sound," Marc whispers, matching his voice to the faint thumps.

Within ten minutes a number of villages have responded to our call, and Marc raises his sticks, takes a deep breath, and pounds the wood for several minutes, sending a message out twice. Everyone glances my way and laughs.

Innocent translates: "We have a hairless mundélé looking for some hair of Mokele-Mbembe. Advice?"

The drummer in Molembé says, "Curse him who goes after the god of the jungle." From Botongo comes a request: "Tell the bald one to bring shotgun shells. We will trade hats for shells." Boha's response is a flat, "We own the lake. Bring money." Boha does control the access to Lake Télé, which lies on the northern edge of their tribal land.

Marc offers me a set of bongos covered in goatskin. Like the larger drums, whose walls vary in thickness to produce different tones, the bongos have tapered sides and have been tuned to a traditional scale. Alain says the drum cavities are crafted with a small adze and a curved chisel; the final minute adjustments are made with a razor blade.

"Are you going to use your hands or do you want drumsticks?" Marc asks.

I take the drumsticks thrust my way. They are carved from lignum vitae and have small balls on their tips.

"Rubber," Alain explains. "You dip the tips like candles until you get the size you want."

I slip the bongos between my knees, trying to recall the technique Maynard G. Krebs displayed on "Dobie Gillis."

"Start out slow. Try to repeat what I play," Marc coaches, rapping out a simple sequence on another set of bongos.

Bong-boom-a-boom-a-bong.

Bong-ga-boom-a-boom-thwap-thud, I reply with my hands.

I try several more times, but my mind seems far ahead of my motor skills. This lack of musical ability has dogged me since childhood, when my piano teacher dismissed me and returned the instruction fee to my parents. Attitude, I assure myself, it's all a matter of attitude. I concentrate, redoubling my effort, but alas I end up whacking my own fingers.

Marc suggests I close my eyes. "Follow the sound . . . Let it start in your gut, not in your head. Let it flow."

Boingga-boom-bonga-dum-thud-thwap. "Dammit."

"Hit the goatskins," someone shouts.

Marc declares my practice session over. It's their turn to play. Marc and Gaspar set up, while Alain adjusts the rusty barrel. At this time of night, the huge village drum is used only to send messages. Alain taps the barrel and counts out, "Un-deux-trois-ah-un-deux . . ."

Alain keeps rhythm while Marc and Gaspar exchange the lead, their arms pumping like teletype keys. Gaspar makes the drum shout with short, frenetic bursts; Marc mixes it up, coaxing his drum to bark or purr, improvising as he goes, his face flashing with emotion.

I suddenly sense the basic flaw in my approach to the bongos. Instead of surrendering to the sound, I was trying to control it; I allowed no room for the drums to speak for themselves. Now, as I relax, my hands magically begin slapping my thighs in perfect time. The music enters my blood. I start dancing, shaking like a wet dog. When the drummers break, releasing me from my joyous trance, I slump to the ground, abruptly reminded of how little I've slept in the last few days.

"Well, you're a better dancer than drummer," Innocent offers. "How come you can't move your hands like your legs?"

A few minutes later I head for the sack. Bidding me good night, Marc plays a special number he dubs "Le Rêve du Dinosaure." The tune follows me back to our house.

I dream of walking through the jungle with my old teacher, Patrick; he smoothes over problems with menacing swamp cats, hissing snakes, and buzzing tsetses; when I'm stumped by the name of an orchid, he's there to rattle off family, genus, and species; we eat what he has gathered in the forest, his expert eye able to sort out the deadly from the delightful.

Patrick was recommended to me by a friend who once worked as a journalist in Africa. "He's the best there is," my friend said. "If anyone can teach you how to stay alive in the jungle, he can." My friend wrote down a telephone number, and I called Patrick, who lives in New York City when he's not in Africa.

We spent many hours together in a basic crash course in jungle survival. Our open-air classroom was Van Cortlandt Park in the Bronx. At night we would retreat to the warm glow of McCann's Bar, and Patrick would spread various field guides out on the bar and continue my education until last call. He gave me a long list of recommended books and made me memorize entire chapters from the field guides and army manuals. He too considered himself the best in the world, and he expected his students to be the second best.

By the end of the ten-day course, I could identify most African snakes and knew the best ways to cook them; I could make a spear out of a tree branch and a crossbow out of a spear, build a snare trap, concoct poisons, and tell the footprint of a duiker from that of a reedbuck.

Snow was falling in the Bronx for our last class. Patrick brought along a colleague to act as an examiner. When I went to shake hands, he threw a stick to the ground and growled, "Snake. Two meters long. Green with a yellow tail and black margins. What is it and what do you do?"

"Green mamba, *Dendroaspis jamesonii*. Keep arms at the sides and move slowly backward. No sudden movements, mambas strike when challenged. Black-snake serum for bites. Four intermuscular and four intramuscular shots in two rings around the bite."

CHAPTER ◆ 14

MY PADDLE HAS BEEN carefully fashioned from the buttress of a plane tree to resemble a palm frond. It is over six feet long, but exceptionally light and flexible; its shaft has been polished and is quite comfortable to grip.

"In Epena all paddlers stand," Gaspar instructs.

"Right," I say, rising to a shaky stance.

Alain casts a nervous glance my way; one awkward movement will send us all swimming. Empty, the pirogue rocks alarmingly in a zephyr; fully loaded, with the weight piled up high, it's even less stable. Fourteen feet long and as slim as a cigar, the pirogue provides speed at the expense of comfort and stability. The boat is an elbow-scraping twenty-one inches wide, and the rails stop just six inches above the water. The bow draws to an abrupt point, good for slicing through reeds and snags, but lousy in quartering seas.

"Very safe . . . very pretty," Gaspar assures me, thumping the sheer.

He stands on the transom, his heels jutting out over the water; as steersman he uses a special oar, longer and thinner than ours. He occasionally sculls with it, but usually it functions as a push pole. In one rhythmic motion, he thrusts the tip down into the bottom, lays his weight into it, pivots to correct course, and pushes off. When we reach the hunting grounds, he alone will move us. Our thick paddles, he announces, are too noisy for the delicate work.

"Watch me," Alain says from the bow, coaching us greenhorns on how to pull a paddle. "It's all in the wrist."

Within twenty minutes the paddling begins to feel automatic. My arms and shoulders become attuned to the paddle; the wood connects me to the river, and I can feel its energy vibrate through the shaft. Balance is no longer a problem as my legs and hips shift automatically as the boat tips. As Innocent observes, "It's easy once you pick up the beat."

"Taisez-vous!" Alain commands. He ships his paddle and drops to a knee, leaning outboard, as his eyes search the shoreline. The pirogue glides along until it loses its momentum and starts a lazy spin downstream. A fish jumps clear of the surface just as a pair of fruit pigeons dart from the forest, brazenly flying inches off our starboard rail, their wings fanning the air around us.

"What did you hear?" Gaspar asks his partner.

"I thought it was the voice, but I'm not so sure anymore." Alain picks up his paddle, and we resume course.

The voice belongs to the river spirit, who sometimes tells him where to fish or hunt for crocodiles. Gaspar can also hear the spirit, but not as well as Alain, who, they say, has a special gift. Alain urges me to listen, noting that sometimes the water god takes an interest in outsiders. "You'll know the voice when you hear it."

"The gods are always talking, but we don't listen enough," Gaspar adds.

We're fortunate to be traveling on the Likouala aux Herbes, he and Alain tell me, because the older the river, the more powerful its spirit. According to them, everything around us is empowered by a spirit, every blade of grass a piece in the giant mosaic. Alain points to a macrolobium tree and tells me that when he concentrates and communes with the tree, he makes contact not only with its spirit but with the whole of nature itself, a divinity that is the sum of all worldly parts. "One spirit leads to another," he says. "The tree moves in the wind and shares the sky; it drinks the water and absorbs the sun . . . and its leaves feed the animals."

Gaspar draws our attention back to the hunt. Up ahead is the giant kapok tree marking the edge of the crocodile hunting grounds. It's an area of mud flats, small islands, and gently sloping banks. "Keep an eye on the tall grass. Crocodiles love it there."

Alain suddenly bends over to scratch his right foot and nervously glances about. I notice he's missing two toes.

"It itches whenever a crocodile is around," he says.

"What happened?" I ask.

"Crocodile. We thought it was dead, but it wasn't. She was guarding her eggs."

Innocent stares at the missing digits and then at me with an accusatory glare. In a whisper, he reminds me that an hour ago we were sitting in the shade, eating chocolate. When Alain invited us to go fishing for "the big one," I convinced the reluctant Innocent to jump aboard. Once under way, we noticed that there weren't any poles or nets in the pirogue, just five spears. In Epena "the big one" means crocodile.

As we leave the kapok tree astern, Gaspar tells us to stow our paddles; he'll pole from here on in. It's not long before we hear a splash about twenty yards downstream, near the left bank. Gaspar swings the boat around and Innocent hands out the spears. Alain smiles and starts pumping his arm, practicing his throw. We drift with the current, moving quietly toward the left bank.

"Merde!" Alain curses as a clawless otter surfaces. It sees us and swims away, its chestnut fur blending into the murky water.

Gaspar points us upstream again, poling silently. Alain remains standing in the bow, holding his spear tip inches above the water. I find myself mesmerized by our reflection undulating in the ripples.

Of the twenty-five known crocodile species, the two most dangerous are the saltwater crocodiles of New Guinea and the freshwater Niles, which inhabit this river. These reptiles are considered the only natural predators of man.

"Which kind of crocodile are we hunting?" I ask.

"The one we see!" Alain answers.

"Big ones or little ones?" The Nile crocodile grows to sixteen feet, but the other five species common to the Likouala aux Herbes rarely exceed eight feet.

"The bigger the better," Alain chimes. "The bigger the skin, the more money. Our biggest was six meters."

"Seven! Not a centimeter shorter," Gaspar corrects.

They use spears not because of tradition or any notion of sportsmanship — they'd use dynamite if they could — but because Gaspar traded away their rifle for a new set of drums. They've speared the giant Nile crocodile before, and they try to assure me that there's nothing to it, despite Alain's missing toes.

Gaspar poles us into a narrow stretch of river walled in by tall mud banks and thorny bushes. The jungle noises sound abnormally loud and chaotic, with a lot of shouting and cackling. For a few anxious moments, I feel trapped in the canoe; I imagine a gallery of predators perched above us, gathering for the feeding hour. Luckily, the banks soon recede as the river widens, but the forest keeps chattering. A troop of green monkeys looses harpy screams, agitating other animals to call louder than ever. Alain says he feels the itching again.

"Hoy . . . up ahead. See the flat grass," Gaspar whispers, exchanging his push pole for a spear. Alain nods.

A small oval of mud rises off the starboard bow. Gaspar carefully pushes the boat forward with his spear, swinging wide and taking us beyond the mound; we'll drift back down with the current. The jungle animals continue to hoot and holler.

Innocent studies his spear, nervously changing his grip, unsure what to do. At either end of the pirogue, Alain and Gaspar stand poised to strike, their feet spread apart, one arm extended for balance, the other holding the spear. Each is focused like an archer zeroing in on the target. I spot the profile of a crocodile several boat lengths away, its head pointed upstream.

Swish! Swish! Two spears zing outboard, their trajectories flat and true.

"Yah!" Gaspar screams, yanking the spear from my hand. I rearm with a paddle.

The beast snaps its head skyward, its powerful tail knocking chunks of the sandbar into the water. It swirls toward the boat, jaws agape. With a startling burst of speed, the crocodile, two spears in its side, lunges for us and flops into the water. Its tail lashes at the river, whipping up a white froth laced with red.

"À gauche . . . À gauche!" Alain orders.

Bad call. The crocodile turns with us. Gaspar abandons the defensive maneuver and prepares to hurl another spear.

Whoosh! The angle is wrong, and the spear skips across the crocodile's back. Innocent tosses him the last spear. The crocodile is closing in fast. The boat is pitching and out of control; Gaspar and Alain struggle to keep their balance. I thrust my paddle deep into the mud and push off with a strength that comes only when a wounded crocodile is pointed at your head. The pirogue shoots forward and stabilizes, but the crocodile's snout keeps pointed at our starboard rail. Innocent joins in, and we push off again.

Alain cocks his arm and fires. His throw is wide. Gaspar wraps both hands around his spear and aims straight down as Innocent and I dig in one more time. "Thuck!" Gaspar lances the beast. The crocodile thrashes by, missing us by inches. There are now two spears in its side and another deep in its neck.

We chase after the misfired spears and keep the pirogue a safe distance from the turbulence. We watch transfixed as the animal repeatedly submerges and surfaces, rolls and hobbyhorses. Blood slicks the water as the crocodile goes limp, its snout under the surface and tail partially curled. Dead, it looks small; in fact, it's only a Congo dwarf crocodile, *Osteolaemus tetraspis*, just six feet long, but we approach with care. Alain squats in the bow, ready with a rope. Gaspar moves forward and cocks his spear, alert for any sign of life. Alain lassoes the jaws without further incident and we tow our catch to shore.

Landing on a mud flat, we drag the carcass out of the water. Gaspar takes out his knife and carefully makes gouges around each spear so Alain can work the barbed tips free. They flip the crocodile to skin it, slowly working their blades, knowing that every unnecessary cut in the hide costs them money. The stench of the guts sends me upwind, but I return to inspect a partially digested duck. Its dark chestnut feathers suggest a Hartlaub's duck. Alain keeps scooping entrails out onto the ground, where clouds of bees and flies swarm them.

"Enough," Alain grunts, brushing the flies away. He turns the carcass over and we drag it into the water. He and Gaspar will finish skinning it under mosquito netting back in Epena.

We follow Alain to high ground, where he digs a hole with a stick, removes a few pawpaw seeds from his juju bag, and drops them into the hole. Gaspar spatters some of the crocodile blood over the seeds before gently tamping the soil and saying a short prayer.

"This will help the spirit find a new home," Gaspar says.

A shoal of butterflies dances in the bilge after we load the crocodile into the pirogue. All but one take off when we climb aboard. It is a small blue from the Lycaenidae family, with black forewings. The butterfly remains perched above the crocodile's left eye, and when it finally decides to fly, it appears to float away, rising straight up without flitting its wings. Alain notices this as well and thinks the crocodile's spirit is being carried heavenward.

"Tokay!" Gaspar shouts, turning the pirogue for home. He starts singing, his baritone voice in tempo with our paddling. Every ninth stroke, Alain calls out, "Yes, yes, of course, yes." Innocent translates the lyrics about a giant bird who delivers food to the sky gods. One day the bird landed without noticing a leopard above it in a tree. As the leopard pounced, a Bantu warrior threw his body over the bird. The leopard bit and clawed the warrior, but the gods wouldn't let him die. Magically, his wounds healed and he broke the leopard's neck.

"Yes, yes, of course, yes," Alain choruses.

When we're halfway to Epena, we hear the Djéké village drum relaying a message about a group of mundélés who have left Boha en route to Epena. It must be the dinosaur-hunting British team, which I first heard about in Brazzaville. The commandant also mentioned that they passed through here on their way to Lake Télé several weeks ago. He had nothing much to report other than, "They came and went . . . Polite men with proper visas."

"They were only here for a day or two and didn't spend much money. They were smarter than you, my friend," Alain recalls. "They brought everything they needed from Impfondo . . . plenty of gas. There were three of them."

"Four," Gaspar interjects. "They kept to themselves. Are you worried that they found Mokele-Mbembe?"

"No, not particularly."

I've been told that the British group has sophisticated equipment and is intent on conducting a scientific investigation of Lake Télé. Although I respect this approach for some things, it's a type of exploration that holds little appeal for me. Being more interested in chasing a dream than in the precise diameter of a footprint, I'm here to substantiate the obscure.

Thankfully, after we beach the boat, Alain and Gaspar refuse further assistance. They'll finish the skinning themselves. As a crowd gathers, Innocent and I leave the hunters basking in the limelight and walk back to our room. When we pass the village produce market, which is usually sold out by eight in the morning, we notice three vendors still standing in the broiling sun.

"Mister! Food here, mister," one dealer says, beckoning.

Dressed only in a tattered jumper, she stands over several rows of rotten produce; the bananas, fermenting inside blackened skins, are bloated and threatening to burst. Her neighbor's yams have shriveled like prunes, and the lemons are brown and mushy.

Innocent takes me aside. Begging, he says, is unthinkable here or in any rural district in the Congo. Instead, the impoverished pretend to have something to sell, and people pretend to buy it from them. The family, not the tribe, village, or state, takes care of those unable to support themselves, and these women must have lost their families.

We buy out the market for six dollars and turn to leave.

"Mister. These belong to you now."

Innocent helps me heap the rotten produce on an old piece of plywood, and we carry it to a village goat pen. The owner of the livestock waves us off, flicking a switch in the air.

"That will ruin tomorrow's milk!" He points to the jungle wall. "Feed it to the ants."

▼

CHAPTER ◆ 15

INNOCENT FINDS ME near the edge of the jungle practicing my drumming on some aluminum cookware.

"You're improving," he encourages, "but, my friend, you still have a long way to go."

He has come to escort me to Gaspar's house, where our host is waiting for us with piles of crocodile meat. We detour to pick up a bottle of scotch and then join about forty people milling about a cookfire at Gaspar's. Everyone but us, still in our hunting attire, wears clean clothing and perfume. People nod politely to me, but I feel as though I'm part of a community outreach program and sense that they would feel more comfortable if I weren't around. At least no one talks about commitments or asks me how I earn my living.

All of the other guests clutch plantain leaves, which, I discover, serve as plate, napkin, and cup. Whenever someone sees the scotch bottle in my hand, they twirl a leaf into a cone and I pour in some liquor. I learn to pinch the bottom of my own leaf cup and not release the pressure.

Alain and Gaspar insist on enhancing the role Innocent and I played in the hunt. It's their party, so they can say what they want. No one seems impressed anyway. We're all here for a free meal and a good time, and when Alain describes the crocodile as an eighteen-foot monster, everyone is polite enough to ignore the puny skin hanging in full view.

The crocodile meat has been chopped into steaks, which some people spear on a stick to roast over the fire, while others flip the meat directly into the flames. A few drop their steaks into boiling water. Innocent and I opt for roasting. The crocodile tastes rather good, but it's very greasy, not unlike tuna packed in heavy oil.

Alain hands me a bowl containing an avocado-colored sauce. "Let the strength of the crocodile be yours. Sip from the brains."

I raise the bowl to my lips, snap my head back, and feel something slither down my throat. Before the taste kicks in, I gulp a mouthful of scotch. The crowd applauds, but it has nothing to do with me: the electricity has come on. There's a burst of activity around the fire as people collect their food before rushing off for the wrestling matches.

"Monsieur mundélé, les autres mundélés sont ici," a young boy announces from under my plantain-leaf plate. The English team has arrived at the village hospitality house, the customary lodging for visitors not escorted by someone like the colonel. When I've finished eating, I head over to meet them.

Since before the formation of the Kongo Kingdom, each village has maintained a public guesthouse to shelter travelers or local families in distress. Often these guesthouses also serve as jails. As the hub of the district, Epena usually has one or two prisoners in lockup, commonly petty crooks caught stealing chickens. Though rare, murder does occur in the district; the commandant told me that two weeks ago his men captured a spurned lover who killed his rival.

The shelter-cum-hoosegow has cement walls and floors covered in a black fungus, and the air reeks of stale urine and bat shit. A rat the size of a pregnant cat crosses my path and squeezes into a hole under the house. Several steps later, I see four white men sprawled on the ground to one side of the building.

"Howdy," I say enthusiastically.

"Hooo!" one of them hoots, shining a flashlight at me. Apparently no one has told them what the drums have been talking about much of the afternoon: the end of one Lake Télé expedition and the start of another.

I try again, this time introducing myself. Three of the four Brits stand to shake hands, but the other remains flat on his back, out like a light.

"He had a rough time of it . . . Bloody hard in spots. More friggin' problems than you want to imagine," says William "Call Me Billy" Gibbons.

Billy and the others flop back to the ground. They're too tired to care where they sleep.

"What are you doing here?" asks Marc Rothermel, the group leader. He looks like someone out of a World War II movie about England's leathernecks. Hearing that I'm about to follow in their footsteps to Lake Télé, Rothermel groans and says something privately to his colleagues. Billy clears his throat and spits.

"Well, did you see it?" I ask, passing out some chocolate bars.

"It?" Rothermel questions.

"Mokele-Mbembe, of course."

"Piss off."

They spent years pulling their expedition together, and

they're not eager to share any hard-earned knowledge. Besides, Rothermel says, "We don't trust Yanks." He goes on to curse the leaders of previous American expeditions, accusing one man in particular of trying to scuttle their operation by smearing their name to Congolese officials.

▼

"One minute we had the friggin' visa, and then we had nothing. The minister revoked it and showed us a letter he received from Chicago saying we were frauds, not qualified . . . It took forever to get that permit back."

"Frankly," Billy says, "you Yanks have been out to get us every step of the way. So who the hell are you?"

I assure them that I'm only a freelancer, with ties to a newspaper but in no way connected to the other American expeditions. They relax a bit after hearing this, yet it takes five minutes of general conversation before they're convinced I won't steal their discoveries to advance my own career as a cryptozoologist. Curiosity, I explain, not advancement in the scientific community has brought me to the Congo.

"Tilting at windmills, eh?" Rothermel concludes. "Christ, mate, you make us look like a top-drawer expedition. I like that."

Rothermel ticks off other expeditions he has been on, in the Andes, Borneo, Madagascar, and South America. All of them were well-financed operations that included numerous field specialists and the most up-to-date equipment. This is the first time he has organized and led a group.

"We're okay. The lads know their plants and animals, but I wish we had better gear."

Surrounding them are watertight camera boxes, bags, and rucksacks containing items I never considered bringing. Influenced by Patrick and Nando, I packed only what I could carry on my back while running: forty pounds. Most of that weight is cameras, film, field guides, rope, and solutions for preserving insects. The Brits, on the other hand, have lugged an inflatable boat and outboard motor; infrared spotting scopes and lenses; a portable darkroom, complete with chemicals and trays; several movie cameras; depth sounders; recording devices of various types; and pricey-looking gizmos packed in fancy cases with double O-ring seals.

The most sophisticated piece of equipment in my kit is a ballpoint pen that writes underwater, prompting Rothermel to try to sell me their used gear. Money is tight, he says, every native has done his part to milk them dry.

"Cheap, cheap, cheap!" he trills, holding up one item after another. I buy a few rolls of film and some water purification tablets.

"Boha is a drag," he cautions, giving me tips about what lies ahead. "But the path to Lake Télé is a cakewalk, less clutter than a Midlands forest."

"What about the swamp?"

"That bit can be rough. Watch out for the mud holes . . . Never saw so many bugs in my life. Mosquito heaven. Ever have malaria? You'll be fine then, the first time is always the worst. Why, I remember when . . ."

Rothermel recounts a few of his many battles with tropical diseases; I've had only malaria, nine years ago. I had run the coastal blockade to deliver a boat to anti-Somoza forces in Nicaragua, but a screwup in communications forced me to hide for a week. Word finally reached Nando, my shore contact and friend, and he rushed to my side, taking charge and leading me over the border into Costa Rica. I felt fine up to the minute the plane lifted off from San José. That's when the chills began sweeping through my perspiring body. Woozy and dripping in sweat, I deplaned in Miami, where customs officials mistook me for a nervous drug runner and strip-searched me. A friend picked me up at a New York airport and drove me directly to a hospital. Six days later I took a cab home.

Rothermel's backpack weighs fifty-five kilos, but he can't

answer a single question about the jungle flora and fauna. "That's not my department, mate," he says. "I shoot 'em and cook 'em. The hunting is good, damned good. Plenty of monkey, snake, lizard, fish . . ."

The Brits spent almost two weeks on the trail and camped half the time alongside Lake Télé, surveying the water currents and depth. The land north and west of the lake, Rothermel assures me, remains unexplored; the guides from Boha refused to leave tribal territory, saying the region was filled with evil spirits.

"What about Mokele-Mbembe?" I ask again.

"That's a laugh. Hey, don't get me wrong. It's a huge forest, and a dinosaur could be out there, but we didn't see one bit of evidence." Rothermel pauses to glance heavenward. The Scorpion lies almost directly overhead. "Look, we're not going to make things up like Agnagna and the Yanks who've been around here."

Marcellin Agnagna is the forestry agent assigned to their expedition. He has accompanied almost every outsider visiting Lake Télé, and he led an all-Congolese expedition in 1983, when he claimed to have sighted Mokele-Mbembe. No one else on the expedition saw the god-beast, and the pictures he took of the dinosaur showed water and flora, but no fauna. The good shots, he later explained to the press, were spoiled because he forgot to remove the camera's lens cap. At the moment he's off visiting a friend in a nearby house, but Rothermel won't be happy until there's a thousand miles separating him from Agnagna.

The first American expedition to reach Lake Télé, in 1981, also claimed to have seen and photographed Mokele-Mbembe. That expedition was led by two Californians, Herman and Kia Regusters, who scheduled a news conference on their return, only to announce to a roomful of journalists, me included, that unfortunately their film had been ruined.

Other American expeditions were mounted in 1980 and 1981 by Roy Mackal, who, as a member of a Loch Ness investigation committee, claims to have seen "Nessie" on a sonar screen. Although he never made it to Lake Télé, he did scour Epena and an area to the south, around Kinami, interviewing people who claimed to have seen Mokele-Mbembe and substantiated previous reports that the dinosaur's favorite food was the fruit of the molombo vine.

A few weeks before I left for the Congo, in February 1986, I met with Mackal at the University of Chicago, where he works. Over the phone he left the impression that he was a full-time university professor, but I found him in the administrative offices associated with the building and grounds department. After we shook hands, he was quick to point out that he does hold a doctorate in biochemistry and has taught college-level courses.

Throughout our afternoon together, he kept calling Mokele-Mbembe "my baby," complaining that other expeditions had "kidnaped" his ideas and discoveries. He was reluctant to share information about the geography, and when I asked for advice on what to pack, he only said, "Take two pairs of Hush Puppies shoes. That's important." He had no doubts about the dinosaur; he was "positive Mokele-Mbembe exists" and read me a few eyewitness accounts he had assembled. He also showed me a plaster cast he had made in Djéké of a footprint the size of a Frisbee. It looked as if it could have been made by a sauropod, but Mackal wasn't certain. He predicted that the Congolese would never issue me a permit, told me to save my money and avoid disappointment, and then sold me a copy of his book on the Loch Ness monster.

Rothermel advises me to concentrate on the Lake Télé area; they found nothing of great interest farther south, in Nboukou and Djéké.

"Don't waste your time or money in Djéké to see the footprint," Rothermel scoffs. "Dinosaur track, my ass. Looked to me like some fancy work with a ball-peen hammer . . . Christ, mate, it's supposed to be the same one Mackal saw in 'eighty-one. Nothing lasts five years in the mud and rain around here."

Leaving the Brits to sleep, I walk down to the riverbank and sit under an oil palm. A fishing owl splashes into the water downstream and screeches victoriously as it whizzes past me. The rhythm of tom-toms and the chattering of jungle nightlife are interrupted now and then by the cheers of the crowd watching the wrestling on television. To my left, on a path to the water, a couple is having a mild argument. She wants him home tonight, but he insists on going fishing. They compromise: she will join him and hold the lantern. They pole off into the darkness, their voices raised softly in song.

CHAPTER ◆ 16

E PENA DISAPPEARS behind the green curtain as we round the first bend. To either side of the motorized pirogue, lianas and aerial roots curl out into the sunlight from the deep shade of mighty balsa, kapok, plane, and barwood trees. Woody herbs tumble down the steep riverbanks, and thin strands of yellow vines dangle above us in the sky. Off to starboard, a seductive flag bush beckons with its delightful red blossoms.

Ahead, the muddy Likouala aux Herbes inhales and exhales, contracting from forty meters to twenty around endless tight curves. As we go, the jungle wall changes as well, touching the water where the banks are steep, then receding into the distance behind the floodplain. The river is calm today; the temperature is already 97 degrees, so Captain Prosper tries to keep us in the shade.

Prosper has been operating the Epena-Boha ferry service since his father's death exactly seven years ago tomorrow. To mark the occasion, the family will visit the gravesite tomorrow morning; three of his sisters who live in villages along the river will make the return trip with him.

"Only the boys remained in Epena," Prosper says, throttling back the twelve-horsepower Johnson outboard so we can hear each other talk. "My sisters had to marry whomever my father brought home for them . . . These days my daughters tell me what to do."

"How old do you think I am?" he asks.

Prosper looks to be in his fifties; his face is leathery and deeply wrinkled, and I know he has six grandchildren with two more on the way.

"Thirty-eight?"

"Close! Two years off," he answers, removing his Coke-bottle glasses so I may correct my assessment.

"Gardez! Gardez!" Innocent cries from the bow.

Prosper whips his glasses back on and jams the helm over to a safer heading. Lowering his voice to a whisper, he confesses, "I have bad eyesight."

He's thinking about changing the name of the boat from *Speedy* to something more fitting. When his father launched her, two men could lift the nineteen-foot hull with ease; today she is waterlogged from stem to stern, and it takes three men just to slide her off a beach. The old outboard can barely push her along. Prosper has an eye out for a suitable replacement; patience though, is paramount.

"Only when you find the right tree do you cut it. Don't rush it. The tree is the important thing."

"What kind of tree?"

He recites the local names for kapok, sterculia, and ambocensis. "Balsa," he condemns, "is no damn good . . . sinks after a few years." He'd love to purchase a boat rather than make one, but that will require some luck in the local lottery. It's a weekly four-number game run by Epena's sole bookie, who pays out $30 to $125, depending on the betting pool.

If Prosper hits the jackpot, he says, "I'll buy a tin bathtub for my wife and an aluminum boat. Something that won't drink water."

Up forward, Innocent chats with Theodore, the newest member of our expedition. We met him yesterday, not long after the police commandant summoned me to his office. The commandant was reviewing his law books during the night and something "jumped out at him."

"Hmmm," he said, inspecting my papers. "You have no Impfondo stamp. All visitors to Epena must have an Impfondo stamp. That's the law, and I must arrest you for illegal entry."

After describing himself as a generous man, the commandant offered me two options. I could sit in a cell until the judge arrived sometime late next week, or I could put up bail. The colonel had left the day before on an extended hunting trip with his brothers, so I couldn't ask him to intervene. I opted to raise bail (a total of fifty dollars), but unadvisedly I demanded a receipt. An hour later Theodore introduced himself. He was assigned to make sure I didn't jump bail. Innocent and I groaned.

"Look, I don't like this any more than you," Theodore fumed. "I'm on the commandant's shit list. You're on the commandant's shit list. And now we are shit together." Changing his tone, he asked us to call him Theo.

Theo is from Brazzaville and has one year left in his army hitch before he returns home and picks up where he left off: "I was real good at doing nothing . . . a pro." Right now he and Innocent are chatting together like old friends, occasionally glancing back at me and laughing. As I try to shift forward to find out what's so humorous, a chunk of rail snaps off in my hand. Prosper wedges the piece back in place, but seconds later it jiggles free and falls into the bilge. Prosper glowers at me.

"Be nice to *Speedy*. She is old, old, old." He blows her several kisses. "She is my friend, my faithful friend."

I stay put and scan the shore for wildlife. There are numerous burrows in the mud bank, but no animals in sight. Exposed rootballs, a favorite haunt of certain bee-eaters and trogons, are empty. What Prosper calls "the happy sound of an engine" must be a tocsin to the river life, sending every creature scurrying for cover. My suggestion to turn off the engine and drift for a while is rejected.

"If I wanted to listen to birds," Prosper announces, "I would have paddled to Boha." He gooses the throttle of the engine he bought several years ago on one of the Congo River barges. Caramel-colored water splashes off the bow and ripples toward the shore. Behind us thousands of tiny bubbles mark our path, popping one by one until there's no trace of us ever passing this way.

Prosper slows down about twenty minutes later and points to the crowns of some oil palms in the distance. "Wherever you see them, you will see men." Groves of palm, citrus, and nut trees mark the villages near the stream and serve as navigational aids. While it's not unusual to see a lone palm or lime in the wild, a grove is always cultivated. Indeed, not once have I sighted a cluster of a single species growing along an uninhabited riverbank. Trees of all types grow side by side, hardwoods abutting softwoods. In the jungle, dispersion of species is the general rule.

Naturalists once saw this spattered arrangement of trees as the rain forest's best defense against the timber industry. It would be far too expensive, they reasoned, to cut away a half-acre of growth to get at one mahogany tree. However, that was before the emergence of the chipboard industry and technical refinements in the manufacture of pulp, plywood, and veneer. Today there's a buck to be made from nearly every tree.

As we clear a tight bend, we're greeted by five men waving wildly from shore. I raise my arm to return their hearty salute, only to have Prosper grab it and order me to help him.

"Allez-y!" he commands as we tilt the shaft of the outboard out of the water.

A thick rope scrapes across *Speedy*'s bottom and pops up just under the propeller.

"Now you can wave. They were swearing before, but now their net is safe."

The fishing net spans the river; one end is staked into the mud of one bank, and the other is cinched to a tree on the opposite bank. Two fishermen dive into the water and swim from the far shore with the rope, which they pass to their comrades. The swimmers stay in knee-deep water as the others start walking upstream, hauling in the net as they go.

"They're closing the gate," Prosper says.

As the shore crew pulls, the net forms an ever tighter loop around the fish; the two men standing in the shallows grope bare-handed for the trapped fish. One fellow shouts and scoops a catfish ashore, where his friends stun it with clubs.

Farther downstream a group of women are washing clothes. Shirts, pants, skirts, dresses, and undergarments are lathered, then twisted tight to be pounded against a tin roofing panel. Beyond them a gang of children playing in the water stop their games to study our vessel as we approach. Seeing my smiling face, they turn their backs and dive underwater.

Prosper slides the pirogue between two others and nudges her bow onto a small beach, the first toll station on the way to Boha.

"Itaka," our skipper announces.

Innocent and Theo jump off the bow. I get ready to debark from the stern when Prosper grabs me. "Deep, deep," he mumbles, and uses a paddle to demonstrate. He dips it all the way in without touching bottom.

"Think, my friend, think before you step," he says, stepping aboard the neighboring pirogue and walking to its bow before jumping.

The chief and the village council are all seated in the shade of soaring palm trees. Drums have long since announced our arrival.

"You're late," the chief pronounces, checking his jeweled wristwatch. "Your gifts will be adequate, won't they?" He checks his fancy timepiece again.

"Yes, sir," I say, handing him four bottles and racing back to the pirogue for two more.

The chief is pleased with our offering of four fifths of bourbon, two of scotch, and a kilo of salt. He and the council hold out their highball glasses, and I fill them to the brim. I toast the village, wishing everyone a long life and a winning number in the lottery. The chief graciously invites us to stay.

"We will kill a goat. Eat and drink and drink some more."

"We have many more villages to visit," Innocent, gentle voice of reason, says, ticking off their names.

"And I must take my sisters back to Epena for the ceremony," Prosper adds.

The chief was a friend of Prosper's father and asks him to stop on the return trip. "We will have flowers and fruit for you to bring to him. He was a good man sometimes."

My Polaroid portraits of the chief and his council are a big hit, and as we're about to shove off, he opens his juju bag and hands me a quarter-inch stainless steel nut.

"It dropped from the sky five years ago . . . landed next to me while I was standing under that lime tree over there." He points to a citrus tree near the riverbank.

The nut most likely fell from an airplane, and once we're under way, Prosper asks if he can have it for his tool kit.

"Stainless steel is hard to find around here."

"Sacrilege!" Theo exclaims. "This has power! I can feel it." I let him keep it, and as he drops it into his juju bag, he says,

"Maybe the gods hold everything together up there with nuts and bolts."

Innocent explains later that the Itaka chief was probably the son of a French political appointee and not the heir to a centuries-old family title.

"He had no scars on his face. A true chief would have scars all over."

Unlike the British Colonial Department, which allowed chiefs to be installed according to local customs, the French Colonial Administration hand-picked most of them and thought nothing of demoting troublesome ones. There were three ranks of chief during the colonial period: chef de village, chef de terre, and chef de province. This three-tiered system invited not only rivalries for the spoils of office but also spying; the divisiveness effectively undercut any unified anti-French nationalist movement.

"It was good for the French, but bad for us," Innocent says, reminding me that the French never developed a competent civil service. When independence finally did come, no one knew how to operate a government; there was neither an infrastructure nor an experienced corps to set one up. "Lucky for us that the Russians and Chinese were around," he says, noting their technical and financial assistance. Their scholarships educated thousands of Congolese, Innocent included. He went to college in Leningrad and studied for his master's degree in forestry at the University of Montpellier in France under a grant from the Communist Workers Party.

Prosper cuts the engine and points off the starboard bow. "Pygmies. Two of them." We glide slowly by the spot, but I don't see them. "Look . . . the gourd under the rubber vine."

White latex drips from a freshly cut liana into a large wooden bowl. My request to stop and investigate is soundly rejected. "Only an idiot would stop," Prosper snaps, turning on the engine again.

"He's right," Theo says. "If you got anywhere near the rubber, they would shoot you . . . poison arrow or dart. That's their rubber, and you leave it alone. Pygmies don't ask questions even after they've killed you."

The Pygmies collect rubber in the forest and trade it, along with jungle fruits, nuts, and herbs, for Bic lighters, knives, and cookware. Over the past ten years a large number of Pygmies have left the forest for the city, and more emigrate every month. Today the largest concentration of Pygmies in the Congo is in Impfondo, not in the forest.

"There's no turning back for them. Once they leave the forest, they've left for life and won't be welcomed back," Theo says, adding, "They have more taboos than we do."

"And we have plenty . . . Catholic priests have been around here for years and years," Prosper says.

A half-hour later, when we arrive in Djéké, I reach out to pull another pirogue close to *Speedy* and step nonchalantly along its keel to the bow. As I leap for shore, Innocent shouts, "Care!" Too late. I sink deep into the chocolate-pudding mud while my companions cross over the next three pirogues before stepping onto solid ground. Prosper shakes his head in disbelief as I slither into the river to rinse. "You're still not thinking," he shouts.

The president of the Djéké village council peers down the steep bank at me. He thought perhaps he had heard the splash of a large fish. He cocks his head, curious about the mundélé washing in the river, but he is polite and asks no questions.

"Stay there, Prosper," the man says. Moments later he glissades like a surfer down the slippery path with a bowl of fruit. "This is for your father. Say hello to him for us tomorrow."

"The drums?" Prosper inquires, wondering how he knew about the anniversary.

"No, your sister, Camille. She wants you to hurry. I'm supposed to accept the mundélé's gifts and tell you not to drink."

Prosper harumphs, grabs a bottle, opens it, and takes a swig. "Everybody, please, drink to my father."

A man shouts from the top of the bank. "Yo-ho. Come to see the dinosaur footprint? I'm your man. I'll lead you to it. Cheap! . . . The footprint is very beautiful."

It's Emmanuel Emugamila, a retired elephant hunter who claims to have seen Mokele-Mbembe three times, once in the nearby Sangha River and twice on the Likouala aux Herbes. He's the man who showed Mackal the footprint in 1981, the same one Rothermel saw last week.

The crew of the *Speedy* confer, and Innocent acts as our spokesman, telling Emmanuel that we plan to stop and hire him on our return trip; right now we're all anxious to reach Boha before dark.

"I'll be here . . . The footprint will be here," he assures us.

A little farther downstream, near a blossoming kapok, its branches studded with the white buttons whose fluff is used in life jackets, we turn off the Likouala aux Herbes and head northward into a sluggish current.

"Bai River," Prosper announces, scooping a handful of the river into *Speedy* and mumbling a short prayer. "The river is a welcome guest aboard this boat."

Innocent rifles through our stores of fresh fruit and hands out limes. One by one, we toss them overboard, each fruit part wish and part offering.

Sangha navigators usually step ashore when they change river courses and pluck a leaf from a tree believed to be tenanted by the guardian of the river. Prosper, a Bakota tribesman, says the Sanghas live in the past, whereas he's a modern, educated man.

"I'm not as superstitious as they are in the far north and west," he tells me.

Several minutes later we sight the first birds we've seen since Epena. A shining blue kingfisher barrels out of the forest and skims along our wake. A yellowtail coucal greedily pecks at a fig vine between glances at our noisy boat; as we close in on it, the coucal puffs its gray-blue chest and darts for the deep cover of the canopy. High overhead, flying a zigzag course, is a pair of superb-sunbirds, *Nectarinia superba*. The male dips its shoulder, showing off its metallic blue-green coloring; the female remains steady, her lemon-yellow feathers gilded by the midafternoon sunshine.

The water of the Bai is a rich brown, almost cocoa, suffused with silt and nutrients leached from the jungle floor. I dip a bug-collecting jar into the stream, raise it to the light, and examine the soupy mix of tiny worms and vegetation. A magnifying glass reveals scores of other worms, larvae, and a few creatures that look like mites. God knows how many life forms are in this one cup of water, and I imagine that a similar broth was once lapped by dinosaurs back in the Cretaceous period.

The numerous large prairies floating down on us keep Prosper on the alert at the helm. One lollapalooza supports a stand of reeds and a twelve-foot-tall willow tree.

"Good fishing," Innocent advises, echoing what I had heard around Stanley Pool.

Every so often Prosper must throttle down as the Bai narrows to a stream only a few yards wide. In these short stretches, Innocent and Theo watch for fallen trees and shallows as I stay ready to tilt the outboard shaft up. Prosper spends these moments cursing the dry season. If, within the next few weeks, it doesn't rain heavily, the Bai will be too low in spots to use a motor.

"I ordered a spare propeller and a box of shear pins five months ago, but nothing arrived except the bill," Prosper laments, adding, "You're lucky, you know. When the poles and paddles come out, my rates go way up."

Innocent grabs the binoculars and focuses on something up ahead. Instinctively, Prosper idles the engine.

"Mud flat?" the skipper asks, pushing his glasses up his nose.

"There's a pirogue up there. Turn off the engine," Innocent says softly. Our momentum carries us silently along. "It doesn't look right. Could be a poacher."

I can barely make out the profile of a small pirogue under a mess of vines overhanging the left bank. Someone has heaped leaves atop the rails and draped lianas over the sides, as if to camouflage it.

Prosper steers for the pirogue as I take out a push pole and try to keep *Speedy* moving — no easy task, I soon discover. Innocent fishes inside his bag and pulls out his forestry badge, a gold shield signifying his senior status in the department. He also dons a set of collar buttons, two gold bars crossing a black circle, the coveted mark of distinguished service and a rare honor for someone not in the military. He pulls rank on Theo and comandeers *Speedy* in the name of the People's Republic of the Congo.

"We're on government business now!" he barks.

"Yes, sir!" Prosper answers.

Theo salutes.

We're about fifteen yards from the other pirogue when the vines above its bow begin to shake; a few seconds pass and we hear the sound of snapping twigs.

"Arrêtez! Arrêtez-la . . ." Innocent commands, standing and raising his fist. "Arrêtez!" he shouts repeatedly. "Forestry agent! . . . Arrêtez! Forestry agent."

Leaves continue to rustle and lianas jiggle, but we can't see who or what is behind them. Theo thinks it's two men; Prosper is sure it's only one. In the distance we can hear the Djéké drum pounding out the news of our boat and crew.

"They knew we were coming." Innocent turns to me. "Push, dammit, push."

When I push us closer, we can see a canvas tarp amidships,

nearly covered by the leaves. I lean into the pole one last time, bringing *Speedy* alongside the pirate pirogue. Innocent grabs hold and yanks back the tarp, exposing a cache of small elephant tusks. He orders the poacher to come forward.

"Last chance," he yells. He turns to Theo and orders him to prepare to fire into the air. Theo salutes again and swings his AK-47 into place, aiming into the treetops.

"Show yourself or we fire!" There's no response.

"Pointez!"

Theo nods, clicks off the safety, brings a shell into the chamber, and lays his cheek against the gunstock.

"Tirez!"

Theo pulls the trigger. Four shots burst from the barrel of the AK-47. "Merde," he says, "I forgot to disengage the automatic."

The forest becomes eerily silent. The gunshots leave a bluish cloud that rises slowly in the calm air. Innocent yells again for the poacher to surrender and takes Polaroids of the ivory. He orders us to probe the river bottom with our push poles.

"They usually throw the big tusks overboard and come back for them later."

Innocent's gold bars were awarded for his efforts to halt the ivory trade. He wrote the federal report on poachers and their industry, and he drew up several sections of the law itself. He's also responsible for reforms that prohibit the killing of gorillas, chimpanzees, and female monkeys of certain endangered species. After years of research on poachers, he's eager to catch this one, but Prosper and Theo wisely advise against going after an armed man in such dense cover. They finally convince Innocent to tow the boat to Ipongui, where he can file a report and alert the police to look out for anyone hitching a ride on the river.

We spend a few more minutes unsuccessfully probing the

bottom for jettisoned ivory, then motor off with the pirogue in tow. When we arrive at the village, Innocent gathers the local council, but the chief says they know nothing about ivory or poachers. His village is peace-loving and law-abiding. The village drummer pounds out an alert, and two councilmen sign the bottom of Innocent's hurriedly written report. The poacher's canoe will stay here, but Prosper will deliver the report and the confiscated ivory to the commandant in Epena.

"Don't you have something good to offer our poor village?" a councilman asks, eyeing the cases of liquor.

We pass out our gifts and stay one drink too long. By the time we're aboard old *Speedy*, we're as tipsy as she is. Innocent and Theo start singing in Lingala as Prosper tries to steer a straight course.

Theo watches me fidget with a camera and stops singing. "Mon dieu," he exclaims, his lower jaw springing out like a cash drawer. "Think of what Mokele-Mbembe is worth . . . just one picture will bring in millions and millions."

He's stumbled onto a disturbing prospect that I've been contemplating for quite some time: the impact on the region if we see and document a living dinosaur. Scientists and tourists would come by the thousands, disturbing the traditional rhythms of life. The ecology could be altered, perhaps disastrously, particularly since the Congolese government, teetering on the brink of bankruptcy, is desperate for new sources of revenue. The lumber companies already clear-cut 145 acres of rain forest a day, and Brazzaville would be quick to build an airfield and hotels near the lake, no doubt leveling miles of trees to make room for them. As Theo and Prosper dream aloud of owning hotels and fleets of boats to ferry tourists, Innocent remains silent. I sense that he shares my apprehension.

"Of course, my friends, you will stay at my hotel for free," Theo promises.

CHAPTER ◆ 17

THE VILLAGE SCHOOLTEACHER greets us from under the sago palms of Boha. Since his name is "As long as a moonless night," he suggests we just call him Teacher. His puffy cheeks suggest an ample build, but it's impossible to tell what lies underneath his voluminous paisley robe. As he moves, the robe balloons and collapses like a working model of a lung. We follow him down a wide laterite path separating two rows of tan brick houses that have rain barrels set under the eaves. Behind the houses are rickety wooden structures of various shapes and sizes. A few have palm-frond roofs, but most are open to the sky and tip precariously one way or another.

"The old houses?" I ask.

"Not old, not new, not houses . . . just kitchens and sheds. Wood doesn't last long around here. Powder-posts are everywhere," Teacher says, referring to powder-post beetles, voracious pests that tunnel through wood, leaving a trail of dust in their wake.

Village women are peeking out at us from behind their curtained doorways, but only the village goats come out to greet us, their nostrils flaring as they sniff my bags.

"What's in there? Fruit?" Theo asks, shooing the goats away as I bend down to unzip the canvas satchel, releasing a sweet smell.

"It's not your clothes," Innocent says from experience.

I remove the T-shirts and discover an unfamiliar package wrapped in plantain leaves, as well as two smaller bundles I didn't pack. Innocent and Theo don't recognize them either.

Inside one bundle are five shotgun shells and a note wishing us luck from Alain, Gaspar, and Marc; the other contains two shotgun shells and two handkerchiefs, with a message from Prosper reminding me to keep my head covered. Innocent peels back the plantain leaves of the large package and finds some mouthwatering pineapple drenched in honey. We eat half of it before I notice the blurred writing on one of the outer leaves.

Innocent manages to decipher a few words: "Thank you . . . brother star . . . father spirit . . ."

I grab the leaf and quickly pocket it.

"Who's it from?"

"A friend." I ask Teacher to give some pineapple to the children playing peek-a-boo behind the rain barrels. My few minutes of enchantment with Monique shall remain private.

The children devour the pineapple, and we resume walking. At the last house on the right, Teacher tells us to wait. He pops inside for several seconds and returns with outstretched arms, palms up. With an exaggerated shrug, he says the village council is meeting inside and will summon us when they're ready. He leaves for the schoolhouse, a long, thin building tucked behind rows of pineapple plants and citrus trees. We pass the time watching the western sky change guard, the gathering forces of purple chasing the pink and gold across the horizon. As the light fades, the jungle sounds intensify; the shrill cry of a black-and-white hornbill is drowned out by the hooting of monkeys, while cicadas begin to trill ceaselessly in the background.

Streams of white smoke rise from the kitchens behind every house. Metal spoons tap against pots, and machetes thunk as they cleave pineapples. Babies stop crying and mothers call their children for dinner. One by one, youngsters emerge from their spy posts around us and dart for home.

We can hear the councilors talking, but neither Innocent nor Theo can understand Bomitaba, the local dialect. Innocent tells me that at one time there were more than a hundred and fifty dialects in the northeast provinces alone. The French tried to banish the native tongues, withholding money and supplies from any village conducting business or running schools in any language but French; after independence, the federal government campaigned to make Lingala the national language, but Boha is still a pocket of the "Old Congo," where tradition apparently means more than certain government subsidies.

"Entrez!" someone says at last, drawing back the thin fabric hanging in the doorway of the council building.

A voice directs us: "A droite . . . A gauche. Arrêtez. Asseyez-vous," as we slip inside.

We sit together against the far wall of a square room devoid of furniture. The packed dirt floor is cool and a bit slimy. The councilors talk among themselves for a while, paying us no attention and rarely even looking at us through the fog of cigarette smoke. The room is lit by a small kerosene lantern suspended overhead. Its cracked chimney casts a spider web of light across the sooty walls. The only decoration is an outdated calendar, compliments of Primus beer, depicting an Alpine winterscape with beer bottles swooshing down a ski trail. Water-stained curtains cover the three windows, and small bones of some type are piled near the doorway. Dirty cocktail glasses are scattered about; three eight-foot-long spears are propped up in a corner, their tips scratching the eaves.

"Do you bring gifts?" asks a tall man with broad shoulders, long sideburns, and an unzipped fly.

"Oui," I say, rising to my feet. "Oui."

Innocent and Theo help me bring in a case of scotch, five kilos of salt, three demijohns of wine, and a liter of brandy. The tall man nods and snatches a bottle with the speed of a lizard's tongue; the others follow suit. The councilors are dressed in tattered plaid or raspberry-colored shirts and black pants. None of them wear shoes, but they all carry juju bags.

The tall man rocks forward on his haunches and says, "I am Ange, president of the People's Village Council of Boha in the People's Republic of the Congo." As he speaks, he reaches out and squeezes my hand with a python grip. Thankfully, a young boy pops through the doorway with a tray of pineapple, and Ange releases my hand before a bone cracks.

"Enchanté," he says softly, and laughs to himself as I attempt to shake off the pain.

One of the councilors uses his shirttail to wipe the cocktail glasses before passing them out. Once Innocent fills them all, I toast the council and the wise people of Boha who have elected them to office. Theo then relates the latest news from Epena, speaking in a mixture of French and Lingala. Innocent, still wearing his badge, interrupts Theo to ask if anyone knows anything about the pirogue filled with ivory.

"Poachers!" Ange exclaims in French with a wry smile. The other men chuckle, shake their heads, and remain silent. Theo resumes his update of regional news and gossip.

The young boy reappears with a tray piled high with some

kind of meat. The man sitting across from me, Gabriel, passes me a small piece. "This is the best," he says, moving closer.

Beneath the charbroil is an undercooked, sinuous pink flesh, greasy like pork and heavily salted. Gabriel watches intently as I nibble at its edges. He has a baby face, with kind eyes and only a few lonely hairs for eyebrows. He's about the same height as Innocent, but considerably thinner. His shirt is missing its buttons, and the back pockets of his pants have been ripped off, exposing his cheeks.

"Tasty, eh?" Gabriel sucks the marrow from the bone. Three of his front teeth are missing, and he slides the bones in and out of the gap.

"It's very chewy," I say.

"This is the last of the monkey," he says, running his fingers in the grease puddled in the wooden tray.

"Oh." In previous travels I've dined on yak, camel, mongoose, dog, snake, rat, even crickets and worms, but I've never eaten this far up the evolutionary chain before.

"When we go to Télé, it's monkey for breakfast, lunch, and dinner. Monkey meat makes up for being away from home." Gabriel licks his fingers and smacks his lips. "Boom," he says, pretending there's a rifle in his hand and a monkey on the rafter.

He asks for a cigarette, and as he flicks the lighter, I recall an ancient Pygmy myth in which chimpanzees, not humans, were the favorite creation of the Almighty God Mugu. The chimps lived in comfort compared to the humans because Mugu had given them the gift of fire. One day some young chimps befriended a Pygmy boy and invited him to visit their village. When the clever boy next visited, he wore a belt made from bark that hung down to his knees. He crouched near the fire while eating a banana, and once the fringe of his belt was red hot, he took off, outrunning the chimps and delivering fire to mankind.

The room hushes as Ange speaks quickly and loudly in Lingala. Innocent interprets, explaining that Ange is addressing the council with a list of grievances about previous expeditions to Lake Télé. Ange believes Boha would be a happier place without Westerners trooping through, demanding outrageous services and then quibbling about the price and the quality of the work. The men of Boha are expert huntsmen and guides, yet Westerners treat them like porters, and forestry agents infuriate them with condescending remarks. The councilmen grunt in agreement.

"He's right," Gabriel says to me. "White men expect us to be like women. They want us to carry the bags, cook, and watch over them like babies. Many times I want to pull the trigger. Boom-boom." This time he points at my head.

Innocent gulps loudly, and Theo nervously glances at his rifle in the corner. I throw back a double scotch and quickly refill every empty glass in sight.

Ange stands and calls the council to order. The People's Council of Boha, he tells me, must decide whether or not we can go to Lake Télé. This is a civil matter, not involving custom or ritual, and the council is the sole arbiter of such cases.

"We establish the rules . . . We assign the guides. If we say yes and let you go, then the chief and the village elders set the fees. First we vote."

"What's to say? I vote no," one man guzzling brandy slurs, then rambles on for five minutes. Innocent deciphers the speech as best he can.

"He's telling everyone how tiring white men are, how they always want the guides to go faster . . . He says white men are crazy, and anyone who comes with us is just as crazy. Not enough money and too much work."

I pour the complainer another brandy and tell him that my gear weighs only twenty kilos; if the council wants, I'll carry it all myself. Ange tells me to shut up and sit down. This is a council meeting; outsiders speak only when spoken to.

"And no one is talking to you, mundélé. Comprenez-vous?"

"Oui, Monsieur President."

A general discussion follows about the lack of food, especially meat, in Boha. While the hunting was good during the British expedition, the men returned home with very little surplus food.

"How many shotgun shells did you bring?" someone asks.

"More than a hundred," Innocent answers. "All of them are yours if we go."

The councilors seem pleased to hear this. A few tip their glasses my way. "Boom-boom . . . boom," Gabriel thunders. One person starts speaking in Bomitaba, and the others follow suit. We watch hand gestures and facial expressions for clues to their conversation. Ange does most of the talking and pauses occasionally to stare at me while shaking either his finger or his head.

"Enough talk. We vote," Ange announces in French.

The yeas outnumber the nays five to two. Ange is the first person to speak after the vote, saying that he will accompany us to Lake Télé. I swallow another scotch.

"Très bien," says everyone but me.

Ange leans toward me and whispers, "I go to keep an eye on you." In a stentorian voice he asks who else will join us on the trail. Previous expeditions to Lake Télé have always had at least a half-dozen guides, but in my case, the first white man to come alone, the council has agreed to change the rule.

"Two more, please," Ange urges.

"I go," Gabriel speaks. He flashes me a smile as he draws a circle in the dirt floor with the jagged tip of a monkey bone, then a circle inside that circle, and so on, until he's made what looks like a target. He jabs the bull's-eye.

"Me," grunts Raymond, a quiet giant who sits in a corner

picking at a half-formed scab on his leg. The wound is the size of a medallion of beef and needs to be cleaned and dressed.

"Let's drink," Theo proposes, uncapping a bottle of Johnny Walker.

Innocent, Ange, and I eventually stagger outside and head toward our room in Teacher's house, leaving Theo behind. We walk three abreast, sucking in the humid air, trying to clear our lungs of tobacco smoke. Overhead the sky is obscured by a thick layer of clouds. Lightning bugs flash, and hordes of mosquitoes buzz around us. The river murmurs as it licks its banks, and a soft breeze is coaxing a whisper from the tree spirits.

"Bonne nuit," a voice calls out of nowhere.

"Bonne nuit," we respond, each of us speaking in a different direction.

CHAPTER ◆ 18

"FUFU?" THE YOUNG WOMAN ASKS as I down the last of my
scrambled eggs.

"Fufu? . . . Qu'est-ce que c'est, fufu?"

Ange told her to serve us breakfast. She's wearing a brown
skirt and a brassiere made for a much larger woman. She has
told me her name, but I can neither pronounce nor remember
it. Innocent is at the river taking a bath, and Theo is still
conked out on our bed of coconut hair.

"Fufu, oui, fufu," she repeats, gesturing to her stomach.

"Me montrez-vous cet fufu?" It might help if I can see what
she's talking about.

She nods and motions for me to follow. We snake along a
narrow path behind the school, pausing for a moment beside
the louvered shutters to listen to the voices of the children
reciting their multiplication tables. Near a narrow field

planted with pineapple, I spot a camwood tree. Its bark is used to make rouge, and its extract is a sweet-smelling additive for coconut oil. I detour to peel off a piece.

"Arrêtez! Diables!" the woman shouts, dashing toward me and yanking my arm.

"Pardon?"

"Diables!"

"Camwood?"

"Regardez!" she snaps, pointing to a row of young saplings stuck in the ground inches from my feet; another step toward the tree and I'd be brushing up against them. "Ça sont taboo! Taboo!"

Later I learn that shoots like these are put in place after a devil has been chased from the village. The spirits of the newly planted trees stand vigil, blocking the devil's return. To trample or damage them would allow the evil spirit back into the village. The devil would have taken residence inside me, looked out at the world through my eyes and attacked any unfortunate soul who looked back. The village witch doctor can cleanse the possessed, but normally the stricken individual runs howling into the jungle before the holy man can perform an exorcism.

My guide holds my hand as we continue down the path, tugging me onward whenever I stop to inspect a hibiscus or try to pinch a flower from a sky vine. Eventually we wend our way to a field that has been carved out of the jungle, its perimeter marked by the now familiar scorched corridor.

Women are working rows of breadfruit and cassava plants, pulling weeds, hoeing and planting shoots. Off to the side, a few women pound roots with massive pestles in a steady and unrelenting cadence. Beads of sweat pop off their ebony bodies.

According to Bantu myth, the women of the Congo are to be thanked for the continued separation of earth and sky.

Once, long ago, the sky god became envious of the earth god's bounty and pressed close to the land. As the heavens descended, drawing the sun dangerously near the earth, the world began to overheat and oceans boiled. The sky god prepared to touch the land, but the women poked its eyes with their pestles and forced the god to retreat. As long as Bantu women continue to use pestles, the myth promises, the sky will keep its distance.

There's not another man to be seen; most likely the males are nursing hangovers or gabbing in the shade of a cottonwood, though a few might be out fishing. Aside from bringing home game and sometimes gathering fruit in the jungle, they do little work. The women tend the fields, raise the children, and maintain the homestead, from fixing the roof to building animal pens. They cook, clean, and serve, as they have for centuries. The future, however, may bring dramatic changes, as the first Boha women travel beyond the district to continue their education. Earlier in the morning, over coffee, Teacher spoke excitedly about two college-bound female students, predicting they would bring home the message of the "people's revolution and free the other women from this forest and snap the chains of the past."

One of the younger women working the fields sees me and whistles exactly like a red-billed shrike. Her co-workers stop what they're doing to gather around me. Those who were hoeing bring their tools, called guindras, with them. Guindras were once a form of currency, and it seems that they're still highly valued. They have short handles and postcard-sized iron blades, often decorated with intricate reliefs of cassava leaves.

"I have come to show him fufu," my guide explains.

"Ah, fufu," they say in unison, tittering.

An elder of the group steps forward. She's wearing a busbus made from yellow cotton with horizontal black stripes. Speaking slowly in French, she explains that cassava (or manioc, as it's commonly called here) roots are left in the ground for up to six months, then soaked in water and eaten as a vegetable.

"L'eau, c'est très important," someone in the group interjects.

"Oui," my instructor confirms, explaining how the bitter manioc must be soaked for at least twenty-four hours to wash out a virulent poison.

Manioc roots left in the ground longer than six months lose their flavor. When these old roots are eventually dug up, the women soak them in water and pound them into an oily pulp, which is then allowed to ferment.

"Ecoutez," my instructor says, picking up a calabash with a cork plugged into its end. She shakes it and holds the gourd next to my ear so I can hear the fizzing.

Several days from now, the foamy liquid will be poured out and allowed to dry in the sun. The solids will be sifted and pounded again. The result is fufu, a flour used in making bread and dumplings. Often, yeast concocted from coconut water is added to the flour for baking pastrylike treats.

There's a cooked loaf of fufu in the shade, near five babies sleeping in a nursery made of freshly cut ferns. Fufu, I soon discover, expands with water, and even a small bite swells to a mouthful. Someone puts a chunk into my pocket and mutters, "Tokay." The women turn on their heels and resume work.

My guide leads me to the path, issuing a warning to avoid the saplings, calling them *orunda*, Lingala for off-limits. She decides to stay behind, and my thanks and good-byes to the other women are lost in the thumping of six-foot-long pestles. I wander back, wondering what vegetables supplemented the local diet of fish and game before the seventeenth century, when the slave traders took human cargo one way and returned from Brazil with plants like cassava, pineapple, potatoes, peanuts, and corn. Arab slavers working the east coast of Africa introduced breadfruit, mangoes, oranges, and rice. Many of these plants have become staples in the Congo; indeed, the only indigenous vegetables I've seen in Epena or Boha are pulses, the generic name for peas and beans, and the spinachlike leaves of certain lianas.

Raymond and Gabriel are outside Teacher's house, caught up in animated discussion with Innocent. Theo is looking on groggy-eyed. The men from Boha, Innocent tells me, are recounting stories of the jungle. For my benefit, Raymond repeats one tale he entitles "The Big Snake." He grabs hold of his spear, which was leaning against the house, and crouches with feet apart, arm cocked, muscles tensed. The incident, he says, took place on the trail to Lake Télé years ago.

"I could hear hisses, but what could I see?"

"Nothing," Gabriel offers in response. Audience participation, I learn, is an integral part of the storyteller's technique.

"There were no branches close to the ground. The birds were singing and something was . . . ?"

"Hissing," Gabriel rasps, and we all hiss.

"I stepped on a log that moved. My feet slid. It was no log. It was a snake that said . . . ?"

We provide the sound effects as Raymond acts out his battle with the giant python, as thick as his thigh and twenty-five feet long. It took six thrusts of his spear blade to sever the serpent's head; even so, he says, the body kept moving, curling around his leg and lashing the ground for several treacherous minutes. He sold the skin to a trader and kept the eyes.

"I ate one and . . ." He pauses to open his juju bag and pulls out a shriveled object. "And with this, I see as well as a python."

Giant pythons have been observed performing mating dances in shallow water, somehow rising on the tips of their tails to undulate high in the air for up to half a minute before flopping back into the water. Could such a lover's ballet have

Open for business: ceremonial spears and a quiver filled with broom cuttings are traditional symbols of power marking the home of a village chief. The empty chair means the chief is in, his office open to all comers.

Congolese children check me out. "Cheap junk, mister," they say, dismissing the pencils, knives, and other catchpenny items I brought to hand out as gifts.

A vegetable dealer sculls downstream as we land at Djéké. It's customary for travelers to stop and pay a toll for safe passage through tribal lands, usually a handful of salt and a gourd of palm wine. We offer kilos of salt and cases of scotch.

After I was arrested, Theo, at left, was assigned to make sure I didn't skip bail. The Brazzaville authorities detailed Innocent to accompany me into the rain forest.

The percussion center of the world: Boha is within paddling distance of Tom-tom and Bongo, and local musicians can coax sweet sounds from almost anything, including rusty fifty-five-gallon barrels and empty aerosol cans.

Two village councilmen and the chief of Boha moments after voting to allow me to proceed with the search for a living dinosaur on their tribal territory.

A Boha councilman prepares villagers for our sendoff down a jungle trail leading to Lake Télé, reputed lair of Mokele-Mbembe.

Our gang: from left to right, Gabriel, Theo, Raymond, Innocent, and Ange.

Ange prepares his pack, made from vanilla-bean vine and philodendron.

This two-foot reptile is a toddler compared to the "grandfather" lizard Raymond hoped to spear. In Zaire there are lizards the size of limousines, called chipekwes.

Butterfly breakthrough: many tropical lepidopterists recommend snake or crocodile meat as a butterfly lure; however, I discovered by chance that a pair of ripe socks left in the sun outperforms all other lures.

How big was it? Raymond uses a stick to describe the width of a giant python he once killed.

Lake Télé is ringed by eleven inlets, each clogged with lily pads and each a perfect nesting spot for a twenty-ton dinosaur.

After a morning of birding, I return to the camp and rush for a camera, sure a brontosaurus has just surfaced, but it is only Innocent bathing.

Lake Télé has changed little in 60 million years. Cycads and tree ferns line the shore, providing shade for air-breathing fish and tree-climbing frogs. It seems one of the likeliest places on earth for a dinosaur sighting.

In the distance a periscope shape cuts through the surface of Lake Télé.

Mokele-Mbembe, perhaps?

Gabriel and I at trail's end.

A diorama sighting of Mokele-Mbembe in Milwaukee.
(David Robbins, Institute of Comedy)

been mistaken for the head and neck of a sauropod like Mokele-Mbembe?

"No, no . . . no!" Raymond and Gabriel say emphatically.

"Mokele-Mbembe is big, big," Gabriel insists, pointing to a plane tree.

"Have either of you seen Mokele-Mbembe?"

They shake their heads. When I ask if anyone from Boha has encountered the god-beast, Raymond shoves a spear into my hand and tells me it's time for some practice.

My only experience with spears occurred long ago in high school, when my roommate tried to show me how to throw a javelin. It soon becomes obvious that my skills haven't improved with age. Innocent isn't much better, missing the target — the trunk of a wild nutmeg tree, *Pycnanthus kombo*, four feet in diameter — again and again. Raymond corrects our stances and shows how and when to shift our weight from one leg to another; Gabriel guides our arms through the proper motion, instructing us to keep our muscles loose as we cock the spear, the shaft brushing our ears and parallel to our feet.

"When you tense and get ready to throw, keep the spear steady . . . Eyes and ears . . . everything at the level of eyes and ears."

The moment of release is most crucial; it's something that can be learned only through practice. The effective range of a spear is only fifteen yards, but Raymond insists that a good spearsman can wound an animal up to fifty yards away. After an hour of practice, Innocent and I start hitting the target once in a while.

The drums start thundering, issuing notice that there will be a village assembly after lunch to hear our petition to visit Lake Télé. Wanting to look my best, I excuse myself to take a bath. Raymond advises me to wash upstream of any villager just standing in the water without soap because "they're taking a shit."

As I trot to the river, a young boy races in front of me and disappears inside the community kiln, which looks like an igloo covered in mud. The boy squats just inside the firebox and stares intently at something in his hand. I bend down, and the youngster inches back into the light, holding open his palm to exhibit a praying mantis. Ange soon joins us. He pats the youngster on the head and says something privately. The boy's eyes light up and he takes off. This is the first time a child under the age of four hasn't cried or fled at the sight of my shiny face and head.

"That was my son," Ange says proudly. "Like me, he doesn't fear white men, but unlike me, he trusts everyone . . . Hurry with your bath. We meet soon."

By the time I return to Teacher's house, children have been let out of school and the women are walking in from the fields. Men are emerging from their houses with chairs above their heads, marching single file down the path like giant two-legged leaf-cutting ants. The furniture is set up in a semicircle in front of the chief's hut, a somewhat inglorious palace of mud, sticks, and woven grasses set close to the jungle wall, separate from the rest of the village. Half the roof is missing, and much of the façade has washed away, exposing its plaited stick construction. A reddish curtain hangs limp in the doorway. The sun is nearing its zenith, piping hot and glaring in the palest blue sky.

When the drums quiet, Ange beckons us to join the conclave. Three chairs have been reserved for us. The village elders are already seated, each at the head of his family. Strung out behind them are their children, grandchildren, great-grandchildren, and, in a few cases, great-great-grandchildren. In Boha it's not unusual to be a grandparent before reaching one's thirtieth birthday, but it's highly unusual to live beyond sixty. The average life expectancy is fifty, with the toughest stretch being the first five years, before the body has developed a resistance to malaria, jungle viruses and parasitic worms. Last night Gabriel told me that he had fathered five children, only one of whom is still alive. Ange has one son and one daughter, his other two children having died within a year of their birth.

The ceremony opens with a prayer led by the village witch doctor, a man named Raymond — no relation to our Raymond — who wears chinos and a short-sleeved shirt with tails that refuse to stay tucked in. At six-foot-four, he's the tallest man in Boha. He has particularly large hands and is endowed with a rich, sonorous voice. Sometimes he speaks in Lingala and sometimes in Bomitaba, rarely using French during the invocation. Innocent translates.

"He's praying for peace and asking the spirits to bless the village."

The witch doctor throws back his head and raises his arms high above his head. His hands claw at the sky.

"He's warning the devils to go away. This is a holy place, and all devils must leave at once."

Taking a shotgun shell and a penknife out of his pocket, Raymond slices into the green plastic casing and empties the powder onto the ground. The elders lean forward in their chairs. The holy man nods to a young boy, who brings out a stick with a wad of cotton stuck to the tip. The witch doctor lights the torch and his voice booms out.

"He's yelling at the evil spirits some more."

The witch doctor holds the torch over the gunpowder and ignites it, sending up a cloud of smoke. The holy man hands off the torch and resumes speaking, his voice mellower.

"The devils have been frightened off . . . Now he speaks about life."

The witch doctor walks toward the chief's hut and seizes a ten-foot-long ceremonial spear with an oversized black iron tip. One fluke is longer than the other, as on a whaler's harpoon. He moves in a slow circle, acknowledging each elder with a short bow.

"He's blessing them and wants them to live as long as baobab trees."

Completing the circle, the witch doctor strikes the ground three times with the butt of his spear. The elders grunt, "Humph!" and snap their fingers.

The witch doctor thrusts the tip of his spear partially into the ground and steps backward. The top-heavy weapon falls in the direction of one elder, who picks up the shaft and returns it to the witch doctor.

The elders snap their fingers.

"The spear has chosen the spokesman. When the time is right, he will ask the questions."

The witch doctor holds the spear in front of him and moves from elder to elder, inviting them to put one hand over his on the wooden shaft. As he moves, he drags the spear tip through the dirt. The moment the circle is completed, he shouts, thumps the earth three times with the spear, and extends one arm toward the chief's hut.

"Humph! Humph!" the elders grunt, and this time everyone but me and Innocent snaps his fingers. The elder next to Theo quiets him with a kick to the shin.

"The circle of life is complete," Innocent explains.

Moments later the chief emerges from his hut dressed in a loincloth and leopard belt. Across his face and chest are vivid slashes of red paint. His lips and neck have been dusted in a white powder. A young boy hurries to his side with a quiver of broom cuttings, the symbol of a chief, and a crudely fashioned crossbow. The chief accepts them, and the boy rushes off to retrieve a spear, which he presents like an acolyte, head bowed and one knee bent. The chief seats himself on a goat-milking stool, surveys the assembly, mutters something, and pounds the ground three times with the spear and twice with his foot.

The elders snap their fingers. The witch doctor fades into

the crowd. People relax, lean toward their neighbors, and speak in whispers. A mason wasp buzzes my face and then lands a few feet away, the sunlight glinting off its blue wings and gold midsection. It gathers mud from the edge of a puddle and prepares to fly off.

Whack! A clod of dirt explodes on my chest. I look up to see Ange gesturing to me from the other side of the gathering.

"I guess that's the signal," Innocent observes.

We carry our gifts of salt and wine and scotch to the feet of the chief, who stares straight ahead, both hands gripping the spear between his legs. Up close, I can see that the red paint traces patterns of scar tissue on his face, shoulders, and chest, sure signs of royalty. The chest scars form elaborate spirals and circles, while those on his shoulders and face are mostly straight lines and rectangles.

The cicatrices are formed by slipping peppercorns under the skin, a ritual normally performed by the village witch doctor when a male heir to the throne is just one year old. Often, if the surgeon has an unsteady hand, driver ants are substituted for sutures: the ants are positioned so that their mandibles clamp down on either side of the incision. The bodies are then severed, leaving the mandibles pinching the skin over the peppercorns.

"Stop staring," Innocent hisses.

We walk backward to our chairs and bow to the chief before sitting. During the ceremony, no one but the witch doctor may turn his back to the chief.

The chief rocks back and forth on his stool and thumps the ground again.

The village elders snap their fingers.

The witch doctor inspects our gifts. He says something to the chief and turns toward the assembly, pointing at our presents with both arms. He approaches the elder chosen by the spear and says, "Oui ou non?"

The elder looks around and nods. "Oui."

"The chief and the elders have accepted our presents," Innocent says. "We are now officially welcome in Boha."

The witch doctor keeps talking as he pulls out his penknife to clean his fingernails.

"He's talking about money now, village fees."

"How much?" I ask.

"Shhh, I'm trying to listen." Innocent cocks his head, and his jaw drops. "Big money . . . They want a half-million francs."

Ange smiles at me as I work through the exchange rate. It comes to almost $2,000.

"What do you say to that?" the witch doctor asks in French, dragging the spear tip through the dirt. An iridescent green beetle scuttles out of the trough.

I confer with Innocent. My French would get us into trouble, and my Lingala, as he knows, is only good for provoking laughter. He agrees, reluctantly, to represent me and asks the elders to reconsider their demands: "The white man comes by himself and asks you to lower the fee."

The witch doctor approaches the chief and says something in his ear. The chief doesn't blink. The holy man retakes center stage and addresses the crowd, his voice rising at the start of each sentence and gradually dipping.

"He says a Belgian expedition paid 250,000 francs, and they only stayed a few days at the lake. He wants us to make an offer."

I know that the British paid only 30,000 francs, plus assorted knickknacks like lighters, knives, cigarettes, compasses, and ponchos. Back in Epena, Rothermel advised me to do what he did: "Bargain, mate, bargain them down. They won't wear you out like Arabs. Just tell them you're broke."

"Innocent, please tell them that I'm poor and . . ."

"No," he declares, cutting me off. "Look at these people

. . . And you want me to say that? Phew! You can come up with something better than that."

I remember my own years of overcharging, back when I lived in a resort community and felt justified in gouging outsiders for work on their fancy yachts.

"Here you go," I say, handing Innocent my wallet. "Let them take what they want."

"Yeah?"

I nod.

Theo grabs my knee. "How will you pay me?"

"I don't know . . . Maybe a camera."

Theo likes the idea.

The witch doctor takes the wallet from Innocent and counts the bills. The elder chosen by the spear examines the contents, whispers to the witch doctor, snaps his finger, and hands the wallet to his neighbor, who also snaps his fingers after flipping through it.

"They're deciding how much they want," Innocent explains.

Across the way, Ange winks at me, Gabriel flashes a smile, and Raymond waves. Slowly the wallet goes from elder to elder, each one snapping his fingers. Once it's back in the hands of the witch doctor, he returns it, grins, and says, "We want 25,000 francs."

"D'accord, merci," Innocent and I say as one. It's only ninety dollars.

Snap! . . . Snap! the fingers applaud, and someone slaps me on the back.

"Eyes forward," Innocent orders.

The witch doctor strides toward us, issues a short bow, and gestures for me to stand.

"Questions?" he demands of the chosen elder, who scans the assembly before pronouncing, "Non."

The witch doctor tells me to sit and lowers his head, speaking quickly, blurting out words without pausing for breath. Once he's finished, he bows toward the chief and raises his head to the sky. Several seconds later, people get up to leave or begin to chat among themselves.

"That's it, all over," Innocent says. "The féticheur asked Mokele-Mbembe not to kill us and thanked everyone for coming. Now we should pay our respects to the chief."

The chief, however, isn't in a mood for talking; in fact, it's difficult to tell what kind of mood he's in. He continues to stare straight ahead as flies hopscotch across his face. The forest is a fully stocked pharmacy of sorts, and I wonder if he's in some drug-induced trance.

"Picture?" I offer, holding out the Polaroid.

He doesn't respond, but a group of bystanders jump at the opportunity and crowd around the stony patriarch. Click! . . . The men whoop as the pictures materialize. The chief, though, remains cataleptic.

"Is he all right?" I ask one of the men.

"Hmmmm," the chief hums, getting up to enter his hut.

"May I ask a few questions?"

"Hmmmmm," he repeats, grabbing a bottle of scotch and disappearing inside his hut.

"Practice, practice." Raymond hands me a spear, and Gabriel tosses one to Innocent, saying, "We leave in the morning."

CHAPTER ◆ 19

A YOUNG WOMAN walks by carrying a bundle on her head. It's white and looks like a loaf of bread. Perhaps it's food she's willing to share. Meeting my inquisitive stare with a smile, she detours our way.

"Manioc . . . I'm starved," Innocent says, rising to his feet.

The young woman shakes her head. "Chalk," she corrects, lowering the bundle and holding it out for us to inspect. The front of her plaid blouse is dusted white. "The chief borrowed it, and I'm returning it to the school." Before leaving, she allows Innocent to carve a sliver from the block, and he gives me and Theo a piece. Nothing happens when I rub the chalk along my forearm.

"Try this," Innocent says, running the chalk back and forth over the grooves in the handle of his field knife. He sprinkles a bit of powdered chalk over my arm and does the same to himself and Theo. The effect of white is barely noticeable on my pale pink skin, but as Innocent notes, "The chalk looks great on black."

Responding to my story about visiting the Fetish Museum and learning about some of the more arcane ritual uses of chalk, Innocent explains that the rites of ancestor worship varied from tribe to tribe. "Only a few tribes used chalk to collect the power of the dead . . . Many more tribes kept a body part, like an eye or an ear, and quite a few saved fingers."

The body parts were considered a family legacy and passed from one generation to the next, father to son. This practice of preserving a piece of the dead was observed primarily in the mountainous areas of the lower Congo and stopped years ago; even so, boxes of withered ears, eyes, and fingers remain in closets and foot lockers throughout the country. Theo recalls how his grandfather wanted to end the tradition once and for all, but he didn't know what to do with the family bag of fingertips.

"There must have been a hundred of them in a suitcase. He couldn't throw them out like trash . . . Finally, he just mailed them off to his younger brother in Pointe-Noire. I have nightmares about them coming back to me, the first son of the first son of the first son."

Today most Congolese believe that the soul vacates the body not long after death and is transmuted into another form that leaves the corpse powerless. "We honor the dead," Innocent says, "but it's the living, our elders, that command respect." Both he and Theo were taught to revere their elders as skilled soldiers in the endless struggle against invasive devils. Their wisdom and experience in battling evil is the family's legacy. Innocent can remember "plain as day" his grandfather standing watch over him when he was a sick child, confronting and banishing the evil that had brought on the fever.

"Maybe the antibiotics cured me, but I'll never know for sure."

Theo excuses himself to retrieve a bottle of scotch, deeming it an appropriate moment to toast our ancestors. Innocent and I lean back and let our eyes drift with the thin clouds coming in from the northeast. The wind is kicking up, and the tree spirits talk for the first time all day. The humidity is near one hundred percent, and the temperature is in the nineties, perfect growing conditions for the fungus in my shoes. Directly above us a colony of weaver birds flit in and out of their cannonball-shaped nests. There are scores of them in one sago palm, and they seem oblivious to our presence, chattering away and fussing with their homes. Below our perch on the riverbank, kingfishers patrol the water, swooping up and down at high speeds. Flycatchers keep to the grass on the far bank, waiting patiently for a meal to buzz by.

"Bonjour," a voice rings out behind us.

It's the witch doctor. He spotted Theo walking with the bottle and glasses and decided to join in our toast. He also wants to ask a favor. The shotgun shell he used in the ceremony was his last, and everyone enjoyed the effect so much, he wants to try it again. I promise him a handful of shells.

"Have you ever seen Mokele-Mbembe?" I venture.

"Oui, tous les jours . . . Mokele-Mbembe is in here," he says, thumping his chest, "and out there in the forest. He is a great spirit, so he is everywhere."

My talk of a living dinosaur doesn't interest him. He believes Mokele-Mbembe is a powerful deity that constantly changes appearance, varying by divine whim and human perception. People have come to him with wildly differing descriptions of Mokele-Mbembe, and he believes them all, sure that no one would risk their own well-being by lying about the gods. Villagers confide in him, but he doubts anyone will talk to us about the god-beast. An encounter with a god is a personal matter that rarely if ever is discussed in public.

I hand him my glass and fill it with spirits.

"Sometimes people say Mokele-Mbembe is small, like a

goat, and sometimes they say he is bigger than the tallest tree
. . . They say he roars and hurts their ears, and they say he can
speak so that only one person can hear him."

He has no desire to meet the supreme forest god face to face.
He's satisfied with the images he conjures of Mokele-Mbembe,
which change shape "like the clouds in the sky." If the situation arose, he wouldn't run from the god-beast.

"I'm too old to run from anything."

Like most witch doctors, he has, over the years, nourished
relationships with specific spirits. Each day he curries their
favor by praying to them and making offerings. In a world
where everything is imbued with a spirit, the witch doctor
must be highly selective in his choice of guardians, and
Mokele-Mbembe isn't one of his.

"The wind god is a special friend, and the river god talks to
me every day."

"Do you think it's all right to look for Mokele-Mbembe?"

He laughs and pours himself another drink. "If the spirit is
missing, you must find it." However, the way outsiders have
been looking for Mokele-Mbembe confounds him. It seems
that some of my predecessors have acted like devotees of the
Church of Gadgetry.

"One man said his metal box would find Mokele-Mbembe
. . . He said the box was his eyes and his ears, and only the box
could prove the existence of Mokele-Mbembe. How is that
possible? And why does he need a box to find a god that is
everywhere? The only instrument to trust is the heart. The
heart, my friends, never lies."

I ask him about chipekwes, the limousine-sized lizards that
have been sighted around the upper Ubangi River. Bernard
Huvelmans, the father of cryptozoology and the author of the
seminal work *On the Trail of the Unknown*, has suggested that
chipekwes and Mokele-Mbembe are but two of numerous
prehistoric creatures still roaming the rain forest. The witch

doctor nods his head. "Oh, yes," he says, he knows all about chipekwes and considers them mighty spirits, like Mokele-Mbembe, but not rivals to the gods of earth, sky, and wind.

"The forest is home to many powerful spirits . . . what you call dinosaurs. They live all around us. Mokele-Mbembe is never far from Boha, and the chipekwe lives in Zaire . . . but they stay away from people and attack intruders. That's why they live in the forest."

"So it's true, Mokele-Mbembe really does kill people!" Theo exclaims. He opens his juju bag, takes out the nut that fell from the sky, and asks the witch doctor to empower it with a special spell. He has heard rumors that Mokele-Mbembe can cast the evil eye, death to anyone meeting its gaze.

The witch doctor returns the nut to Theo and reminds him of the difference between an intruder and a guest. No one, he cautions, should enter the jungle without first communing with the more powerful forest spirits. While some gods are more tolerant than others, all have their limits and will rebuke insolent mortals who violate them, unleashing devils to do the dirty work. A minor offense may change a man's luck for a certain amount of time; major offenses bring disease or death. Not being in daily communion with Mokele-Mbembe, the witch doctor can't predict how the god-beast will react to us. However, he's confident that the jungle deity isn't an evil spirit, and in any case the god of wind will watch over us.

"If there's danger, the wind will blow the danger away," he assures us.

The sound of drums erupts behind us. A column of smoke rises from the far end of the village. People emerge from their houses, and someone shouts for us to join them at the fire. We linger for a while, sipping the last of our drinks. The waxing moon is visible now, a faint imperfect circle climbing slowly into the night. Off to the west, the last of the sun is melting into the treetops. The witch doctor stands, looks northward, and holds out his arms, pointing at the two astral orbs.

"Tomorrow you will walk between the sun and the moon . . . to where Lake Télé lies. If I was younger, I would go with you. I'm told the fishing is still good."

The smoke is coming from near the council house. Women are dancing to an array of percussive instruments, from traditional drums to pots, pans, and empty aerosol cans. One man plays the sweet-sounding *m'bichi*, a thumb organ made from metal strips attached to a sounding board. The women dance and sway at one end of the fire, and the men stand together at the other. I wonder if this is the leopard dance, held once a year, a ritual event staged by the village women, who pretend they're leopards; the young girls chase them off, protecting the men from attack.

Innocent checks with a bystander. "They're celebrating first blood. A girl has become a woman today," he says, explaining that it's a spontaneous party, whereas the leopard dance comes at the end of a three-day celebration of womanhood.

An elder spots me in the crowd and waves. After taking a swig of scotch, he circles the fire twice and spits a bit of liquor over the flames, which sizzle and smoke.

"All praise Mokele-Mbembe," the elder intones. "He is great. He is big. He is powerful."

I lean toward the witch doctor to ask a question, but before I can speak, people start shouting and applauding. The young woman we're honoring tonight has just appeared with her mother. The two of them start dancing, dressed only in grass skirts dyed red and brown from vegetable extracts. Other women soon join them. Gourds filled with palm wine appear and are passed around.

"Could Mokele-Mbembe be a female spirit, a goddess?" I ask the witch doctor.

He shudders and shakes his head. "The father creates his son."

"But it's possible, isn't it?"

"No, no way," he avers, and turns to bless the young woman, whom he introduces to the crowd as the future of Boha.

CHAPTER ◆ 20

OUR DEPARTURE IS SET for ten in the morning, but I'm awake well before dawn. It was easy to nod off last night, but impossible to stay asleep. The clapping of a loose shutter, the wind in the branches, and the odd noises from the jungle all disturbed my slumber. I sat up and tried to identify some of the nocturnal sounds, but soon gave up, distracted by the loud snoring of Innocent and Theo and by the drizzle tapping on the metal roof and dripping, drop by drop, into the rain barrels.

I pull out my notes from the Van Cortlandt School of Jungle Survival and try to read them by flashlight. Instead of reassuring me, the notes remind me how little I actually know about the jungle. My ten-day crash course in the Bronx doesn't seem like much now; my only real experiences in tropical exploration have been four day trips through Central American rain forests, with Nando, my guide, telling me when to move, what to eat, and where to sleep. I did little more than follow instructions and carry my own gear.

Here I'll be trekking with five men through an uncharted rain forest. We expect to be gone for nearly a month, hunting and foraging for food and drinking water where we find it. I hope no one is relying on me to do much hunting. I gave that up when I was nine, moments after dropping a squirrel with my Daisy BB gun. I was so distressed by what I'd done that I dug a grave, filched a cupful of holy water from the parish church, baptized the squirrel, and buried it in one of my mother's best linen napkins. Later, in an archery class at summer camp, I was the only one required to wear steel-tipped safety shoes. I'm pretty handy with a slingshot, but my skill lies in shattering street lamps and bottles, not moving targets.

Flicking on the flashlight again, I return to my notes, reading the section headed: "Green and black snakes."

mambas strike w/ whiplash motion; vipers hit like sledge-hammers . . . Alive 3 hrs. post mamba bite = clear sailing; viper bite deceptive, poison (anticoagulant) may cause int. hemorrhaging, check stool & urine for blood, monitor pulse.

"What are you doing? Reading at this hour?" Innocent asks, wiping the sleep from his eyes.

"Oh, just going over some things."

"I'm having strange dreams. How about you?"

"Nah, slept like a rock," I lie.

A few hours later, Innocent and I are drinking tea when Theo returns from his morning constitutional. The village health officer is outside, watching to make sure we use the outhouses.

"Throw a rock inside before you go in," Theo advises as I head for the facilities.

We've avoided the outhouses in Boha so far, and I've never seen any of the villagers use them. In Epena there were a half-dozen well-maintained toilets, with barrels of lime outside each door, but in Boha creepers have swallowed the rust-covered pails next to the two outhouses, which are set off by themselves near the jungle wall. I knock on the door.

"Bonjour? . . . Bonjour?"

There's no response, but when I open the door, an angry swarm of bees rushes out, along with a noxious odor. I jump backward as the door snaps closed on its spring hinges and pepper the outhouse with dirt bombs until the bees stop coming out. What's a few bees to someone about to explore a pathless jungle? No problem, I tell myself, and step boldly inside. As I squat over the hole, I can barely see the walls in the dim light. Something keeps dropping on my head, so I crack open the door to find that the inside of the outhouse is caked with wriggling, oozing maggots. I jump up, trying to pull on my pants, and spring outside, landing bare-assed in a heap on the ground.

"Mon Dieu!" Innocent exclaims. He elects to use the other outhouse, but once again a swarm of bees curls out. Regardless of what the health officer has to say, Innocent stalks off into the jungle to relieve himself.

Teacher tells me later that the poor condition of the outhouses isn't the fault of the village but of the regional government in Impfondo. Lime and disinfectant are supposed to arrive the first of every month, but they haven't had a shipment since last year. The village council writes to complain every other week and gets a letter back each time promising action.

By ten o'clock we're almost ready to move out. Food and communal gear, like the flashlights and liquor and ammunition, are spread across the ground and are slowly being arranged by Raymond into six equal piles, none of which will weigh more than twenty pounds. Each of us carries his own personal items, with Gabriel's kit the lightest of all — only a mirror and a toothbrush.

The witch doctor sings as he approaches us, "I've been praying for you."

"Merci."

"The wind god will protect you . . . and I believe Mokele-Mbembe has listened to me as well." The witch doctor looks at me and adds, "But we still have some work to do . . . You must be cleansed. Lake Télé is sacred to us."

Recalling my last spiritual cleansing, I ask if we can move into the shade. "Bien sûr," he agrees and suggests a large lime tree across the way, where we surprise Teacher's wife. She's gathering the white flowers form a nearby pyrethrum bush.

"Insects," she says, waving an arm through the air. When the pyrethrum flowers dry, she'll either burn them to chase away mosquitoes or grind them into a powder, a natural insecticide.

Once she slips back inside her house, the witch doctor looks around and, finding no women in sight, nods. Women shouldn't witness the cleansing of a male, and vice versa.

"Each has secrets that must be protected."

I start to take off my shirt, but he stops me. If spirits can pass through the bark of an ironwood tree, surely they can pass through your clothing.

"Just stand there and think about the wind god and the forest god, Mokele-Mbembe."

He pours some water from a canteen into his palm and anoints me while reciting a short prayer. He repeats the prayer as he gathers a handful of dirt and lets it sift through his fingers onto my feet. He then blows softly into my left ear.

"Très bon," he announces, satisfied.

"C'est tout?"

"Oui," he replies. "I have loaned you a powerful spirit and asked the gods to watch over you. What more can I do?"

The witch doctor sends word to the village drummer to

announce our departure. The message goes out, and moments later we hear replies from other villages.

"What's the word?"

"Better than before," Innocent says, cupping his ear. "Only one village is denouncing you. American go home, they say."

"Good idea," Ange growls.

CHAPTER ◆ 21

T HE SCHOOL BELL CHIMES an early recess, and children
scramble from their classrooms. Women return from the
manioc fields or the river, while men hotbox their cigarettes
down to the nub and rise from their chairs in the shade to see
us off.

A woman comes up to me with a string of rosary beads in
one hand and a fetish in the other. She rubs each along my
forearm, first using the plastic cross and then a tiny red doll,
which has a brass thumbtack stuck between its painted eyes.

"Good spirits. They bring luck and good hunting," she says,
pressing the cross into the doll's face, then walking off into the
crowd. Ange smiles at the woman and she rubs his forearm as
well. Gabriel and Raymond line up behind Ange for their
blessing. Innocent tells me that the first Portuguese sailors to
visit the Congo exchanged rosary beads, talismans, and holy

relics for native dolls. The Western charms were called *feitico* in old Portuguese, and that led to the dolls being called fetishes.

"Play something for the wind spirit," the witch doctor instructs the drummer.

He responds with an up-tempo rhythm, and several men dash to their houses and return with instruments. They join the village drummer, layering the music and driving the melody forward. The young man next to me pounds his bongos with a bone of some type.

"Bongo, naturellement!" he says, slapping his leg to indicate where on the animal it came from.

The witch doctor stands in the middle of the path, tapping the shaft of his ceremonial spear, one of three in Boha. The vice president of the village council stands next to him, holding the second spear. The chief owns the third, but I don't see him around. Teacher is all excited, speaking rapidly in French, Lingala, and English, telling me that his daughter's temperature is down and her appetite has returned. "For the medicine you gave her," Teacher says, stuffing something into my shirt pocket. It's a coin purse made from lizard skin. Inside are all types of seeds. "Plant them and their spirits will thank and protect you."

"Oui?"

"Oui," the witch doctor confirms.

We shoulder our bags and take up positions behind the witch doctor and the vice president. Out of the corner of my eye, I spot the chief lurking in the doorway of his hut, and I wave to him. He doesn't respond. The witch doctor raises his spear, and the music comes to an abrupt halt.

"Tokay," the witch doctor announces.

The villagers spread out to either side as we pass, and a few wish us good hunting. The woman with the fetish and rosary beads has her eyes closed, but her lips are moving, no doubt praying for us to return with plenty of meat.

No one follows us beyond the school, where we veer to the right, avoiding the devil's path near the camwood, and enter the manioc field. Halfway across the field, the witch doctor and the councilor step out of the procession without saying a word. At the edge of the forest we stop to adjust our bags. While the others fidget with their gear, I run my hand over the belly of the jungle wall, which bulges out several feet, like the topsides of a mighty ark. The wall's rough exterior is woven from a jumble of tightly knit vines, forming a warp and woof that defies my attempts to separate them. Stepping back, I note an unusual number of parasol trees, a sure sign that this is second-growth jungle. Maybe it's a part of the original manioc field that has been reclaimed by the forest. Parasols, or umbrella trees as they're often called, are pioneers, speedy growers that are always among the first to establish themselves in a new clearing. They can grow up to eight feet a year for the first ten years, but such prodigious growth comes at a high price. Parasols die young, crashing to the ground by their eighteenth birthday, rotted by fungus and strangled at the roots by the dominant trees, like mahogany and djave nut, slow and steady growers that live many centuries.

In an area dappled by sunshine I plant several of the seeds Teacher gave me, placing them away from the tended rows of manioc, where they might be mistaken for weeds. Raymond helps me plant them and instructs me to blow into the soil on top of each one. "The breath of life," he explains. Gabriel loads his Chinese-made shotgun and asks us to stand back.

"For luck . . . We fire once before we leave and once when we come back. See that fig vine over there? Make sure you touch it three times before going inside."

He aims into the jungle and pulls the trigger with the gunstock inches from his shoulder. The recoil kicks the barrel up, sending the shot high into the canopy. He stares accusingly at the shotgun for several seconds, and rubs the barrel with an arum leaf.

"I'm waking the spirit," he says, reasoning that the shot went high because the gun spirit had been asleep. It has been weeks since he last fired the gun. "You're awake now, aren't you?" he asks the spirit, holding the weapon to his ear and apparently satisfied with what he hears.

"Follow me," Ange exclaims, taking the lead. We string out behind him, each of us tapping the lucky vine.

We sidle through a slot in the jungle wall, stepping over plants pushing up from the ground and hunching under overhanging limbs and vines. The ambient light diminishes with each step. No place on earth has more flora per square foot than a second-growth jungle; it's a chaos of runners, creepers, trees, bushes, and herbs, many spiraling in death grips around the others. Over time the vegetation will settle into a hierarchy headed by the dominant trees, but until then, passage must be earned with endless whacks of a machete. Someone in front of me curses; we remain crouched in the semidarkness listening until a voice says, "Tokay."

"Reach out," Gabriel orders, and grabs my shoulder.

I latch onto a sleeve.

"Not me . . . Behind you!"

I grope for Innocent, but he swats my hand away. "I thought it was a snake," he says, telling me to keep my hands to myself. On we go, wiggling through vegetation that sustains itself in less light than I can read by.

Several minutes later, on the other side of the wall, we spring upright intruders in an emerald world domed by leaves, vines, and limbs. Now there's no need for high-stepping or hunching; the primeval tropical forest is remarkably uncluttered, with less underbrush than in a temperate forest. We can see for hundreds of feet in almost every direction.

I stretch toward the bottle-green sky. At last I've entered Mokele-Mbembe's domain: a pristine world where plants are kings and dinosaurs gods. While the rest of the earth has undergone dramatic geological changes, this steamy chunk of Africa has remained in the Cretaceous period, the sunset years of the dinosaur hegemony. Winter was unknown, and mammals were just emerging into a world populated by spiders, scorpions, and reptiles. Trader Horn once described Africa as a place where the past has hardly stopped breathing; but in the Congo jungle, it seems that the past is indistinguishable from the present. My surroundings look as if they've been lifted from a diorama at a natural history museum. The first creature I see is a dragonfly, another survivor from the dinosaur age. I call out to Innocent, wanting him to see the double-winged insect with ruby eyes.

"Shhh!" Gabriel admonishes as he looks above.

"Monkey," Ange whispers, directing my attention to a tree several hundred feet away. With my binoculars, I make out the profile of a green monkey.

It's a difficult target even for an accomplished marksman, but Gabriel has faith in his gun spirit, and the sight of a monkey makes his mouth water. Lucky for the olive-furred simian scampering along the high branches that he's such a poor shot.

"Huh, the gun spirit must be mad at me," Gabriel says after missing. Again he plucks a leaf and rubs it along the barrel; this time he talks at length to the spirit, urging it to guide his future shots.

It's almost high noon, yet we're bathed in diffused light. Many details that would be lost in bright sunshine, like the pale yellow lines on the leaves of variegated palms, are beautifully radiant. Most of the tallest trees are entwined with climbing vines or draped with aerial roots. One impressive plane tree draws my attention. Its trunk is a round, barely tapered column, like a factory smokestack, vaulting twelve stories into a thick haze of leaves. At its base are four massive buttresses, with ample space between them to park a station wagon. The others help me measure its girth with a fishing line. Its circumference exceeds twenty-six feet.

"Small boy," Gabriel scoffs. "The grandfathers live near the lake. They are twice as big."

"This is where life started, you know," Raymond says. "Right here under a plane tree . . . love began."

"Pardon?"

"The forest came before people," he explains, "until one day a rose apple fell from the claws of an eagle and landed on a buttress of a plane tree. The apple split in two. A man grew from one half and a woman from the other . . . That's what the Pygmies say."

"That's what the priests say the Pygmies say," Ange interjects. His favorite story as a child was "a real Pygmy story" about creation. "It all started in a night world . . . Before there were forests, there was only darkness . . . ." The gods grew bored with this dark universe and decided to create a diversion. They ordered astral mud wasps to build a giant nest, earth, out of black matter; worms were then commanded to fertilize the soil, and their burrowing created mountains, valleys, and riverbeds; at the same time, fireflies were assembled to form the sun, moon, and stars.

"Then," Ange says, grabbing a handful of humus, "the gods blessed earth. They gave us water. They gave us trees. They gave us life."

The men from Boha stride northward; they've walked this route often and can't understand why I'm constantly checking my compass.

"Only idiots get lost," Ange says flatly.

He demonstrates the first rule of trail blazing, slashing a tree with his machete and bending the stalk of a waxy arum plant to the ground. "If we do that every twenty or thirty meters, no one will get lost . . . and don't forget your whistles." We each carry a plastic whistle to signal those out of eyeshot.

Innocent and I lag behind the others, more interested in studying the plant life than in listening to the hunters talk about past monkey kills. Like confused doctors standing over a patient, we pinch and probe plants, take notes and cuttings, and flip through reference books trying to identify species. At first glance, almost every tree looks like a twin of the one closest to it. All have leathery green ovate leaves, smooth light-colored bark, and trunks that rise straight and true. But slowly we learn to discern one species from another, relying not only on our eyes but also on our noses and fingers. Jabbing a knife into the cortex can release the pungent essence of the tree, and running a hand over the bark can reveal subtle differences in texture that escape the eye.

At the base of a patternwood tree I notice a vine that looks familiar. Matching it to a picture in the field guide, I determine that it's a philodendron, a cousin of the plant that grew in the corner of my old office in New York. However, this gigantean version is seventy feet tall. If only it were a strangler species, I would take a cutting back to give to my former boss.

We hear the sound of a whistle, but we can't find our own to respond — or even our bags. We put them down while we collected plants, and we locate them just as Ange arrives, huffing and puffing. He thought we might be in trouble, but as he says with a sneer, "*You're* the trouble."

He's anxious to reach tonight's campsite and begin stalking game, so we walk double-time to catch up with the others. Innocent and I may be after plants and dinosaurs, but Ange is after meat. Once we're reunited with the group, Raymond volunteers to shepherd Innocent and me while the others push on. After the forest warriors leave, Raymond tells us that he prefers a leisurely pace. "I don't like to rush anywhere." He adds, "The tortoise, you know, always has something to teach the spider."

As the three of us stroll along, I concentrate on the smells of the forest. There are raw odors of decay, sweet fragrances of new growth, potent swirls of methane, musky perfumes, and alluring scents of nectar. Each breath has a different taste from the last, some bitter, some sweet. Kick up the leaf clutter and a stench arises; jostle an orchid and volatile oils excite the air; squeeze a blossom and pollen sprays a honeyed mist; snap a root and earthy aromas circulate.

With the air saturated with moisture, there's little evaporation, and each drop of sweat soaks me further, attracting bees, flies, mosquitoes, and clouds of tiny gnats. The rubber bands cinching my cuffs don't deter the ants from marching up to my torso, and spiders drop from overhead or scurry across my face when I walk through a web. Skin borers, a problem in Epena, are a plague here. They drill into my arms and hands, some burrowing to their deaths, others finding a new home in my bloodstream. Pollen glazes me like a baked ham.

Insects chatter all around us, a bluster of clicks, whirrs, trills, and cheeps. Right now, in the middle of the afternoon, most mammals and birds are quiet, though the hornbills and touracos keep calling, as they will throughout the day and night. Several times reptilian hissing noises sizzle through the air, and I change course quickly. In the background is the constant splattering of water drops and detritus falling from leaf to leaf, from canopy to floor, an omnipresent sound generated by condensation and by millions of arboreal creatures going about their business. The forest is worked twenty-four hours a day, with some animals on the night shift, others on the day shift, and still more, like certain saprophytes, that do their char work around the clock.

The jungle is a triple-tiered world sustained by abundant rainfall and relatively constant temperature. Far above me, almost two hundred feet overhead, is the luminous upper canopy, formed by huge trees with immense flattened crowns. Although the canopy appears seamless from the ground, each crown is actually circled by a meter-wide halo of air. Birds use these gaps as doorways to the sky; botanists believe they are a defensive mechanism that prevents flightless insects on one tree from infesting a neighbor.

The major branches of these giant trees, usually four or five in number, are draped with hundreds of multicolored vines, some wide and others narrow, like a great tie rack. These are epiphytes, which have no roots on the ground. They live off the debris that accumulates in the canopy, and many of them draw moisture from the air through the spongy outer covering, or velamen, of their aerial roots. While most vines grow straight down, others spiral, curl, and arc up and down in an endless variety of rococo patterns. The ones that need the most light, especially orchids and aroids, prosper in the high forks and crooks.

Rain forest trees blossom at all times of the year, and not all flower annually. The energy involved in producing pollen, millions of seeds, and thousands of fruits (a mass of new growth often weighing more than a ton) can exhaust one of these giants; depending on soil conditions, it may take two or three years to replenish the nutrients needed to blossom.

Parrots, coucals, bulbuls, barbets, warblers, babblers, sunbirds, flycatchers, finches, and several hundred more species of birds build their nests and patrol for food in the canopy. Because of the huge diversity and sheer number of trees, there are always fruits and insects to eat. Raptors cruise above the canopy in search of prey; some eagles feed on monkeys twice their size.

Monkeys, more than twenty species of them, including mangabeys, guenons, monas, Dianas, patas, and thumbless colobuses, share the upper canopy with birds, snakes, frogs, and countless insects. The monkeys usually move through the canopy in troops, returning to one dormitory tree night after night until they've picked an area clean. Various prosimians, wet-nosed cousins of the monkey, also live up there. Mainly nocturnal, they have the best night vision of any animals in the jungle, thanks to a crystalline disk behind the retina that reflects light back onto the lens. Although they're never credited in patent applications, prosimian eyes are the models for modern telescopes and night scopes.

The second tier of the rain forest, the middle canopy, is a world of oval-crowned trees, fifty to a hundred feet high, that sop up what sunlight manages to filter down. Many of these trees are future giants biding their time until age or disease fells an elder overhead. Once they gain access to direct sunlight and have room for root expansion, they supercharge and spurt skyward. How long a tree will have to wait, or even how old it might be, is difficult to tell in the tropics. Since the forest is seasonless, there are no annual sap surges and consequently no rings to count. Laboratory tests suggest that the lifespan of a baobab exceeds 4,500 years, and botanists suspect that some other species outlive them. Right now, though, no one is even sure how many different kinds of trees grow in the rain forest; estimates vary between 2,500 and 4,000.

The middle-canopy trees are also host to a boggling array of epiphytes. To my left is a mammee apple tree, its trunk barely visible behind the curtain of vines hanging from its branches. I slash at a few of the aerial roots. One vine in the Apocynaceae family starts dripping a white latex, and I collect a few drops of the natural rubber for my collection. A neighboring vine yields several cups of crystal-clear water, but I double-check my field guide to make sure it's in the Buettneria family before taking a sip. Another vine oozes a clear liquid that drips on some leaf-cutting ants. Within seconds, the ants drop their burdens, race wildly about, and die.

As we amble northward, I keep noticing clumps of leaves in the branches of the middle-canopy; more than likely they're nests belonging to one of the many medium-sized mammals, such as chimps, leopards, and swamp cats, that sleep or roam in this tier. The middle forest is also the favorite haunt of pythons and mambas and of what sound like the loudest frogs in the world, including one species with a call not unlike someone sitting on a whoopee cushion. Lord Derby squirrels live here as well. They're the best fliers among mammals, equipped with a gliding membrane that acts as a sail, allowing them to soar more than a hundred yards through the air.

The third tier, the shrub layer, where I stand unable to see the sun, is carpeted in fallen debris. The trees here are rarely taller than fifteen feet and have spindly trunks with few leaves. They, too, are waiting their chance to move up, ready to fill any vacated niche in the middle canopy. But the majority of plants in the shrub layer are herbaceous, with varieties of ginger, arum, and arrowroot predominating. Many of their leaves are tinted a faint yellow, purple, or red, from excessive carotene and xanthophyll, which the plants produce to better utilize the available light.

Among the large animals that inhabit the ground level are lowland gorillas, jungle elephants, and hippopotamuses; smaller residents are rats, rabbits, pangolins, porcupines, mongooses, snails, tortoises, and of course insects. A day's march from here, we will enter an area dotted by tiny lakes, pools, and swamps — the home ground of bushbucks, sitatungas, and bongos, large ungulates the size of cattle, with long, twisted horns. Fleet-footed and with a mean kick, they fear only humans and leopards. If we're lucky, we might spot an okapi, which, like Mokele-Mbembe, was considered a creature of the imagination until one was caught in the early 1900s. Descended from the giraffe, the okapi has striped legs that hoist it almost seven feet in the air.

On the ground grow many saprophytes, the most obvious of which are mushrooms and other fungi. Unable to produce their own food, as green plants do, saprophytes derive nourishment from decaying matter and come in an array of outrageous colors: livid reds, poison yellows, and violets. Stinkhorns, also known as "dead man's fingers," pop up here and there along the trail. Phallus-shaped, with blood-colored splotches, stinkhorns smell like feces, a perfume to the flies that the plant relies on to disperse its spores.

"Whirr-woo-wuuu," Raymond calls. "Whirr-woo-wuuu."

He's standing next to a mahogany tree with his spear pointed at a hole under a buttress. Following his instructions, I clear away the leaves and gently probe the shallow burrow with a stick. Feeling something, I fall to one knee to scoop out more debris. Two bright orange eyes stare out at me. Further enlarging the hole, I get a clear look at a long-nosed mongoose, baring its teeth and snarling. My friendly cooing sound makes it snip at my fingers. I reel backward, bumping into Raymond as the mongoose flies out of the hole and darts up a nearby tree, its tail high in the air. Raymond regains his balance and goes in hot pursuit, but he's no match for the swift climbing creature.

"Next time," Raymond announces, narrowing his eyes, "you stay away and Innocent helps me."

An hour later we see smoke from the campfire and come upon Theo fanning a few hot coals with a blowpipe fashioned from a hollow liana. He says that Ange and Gabriel are off hunting monkey. Raymond grabs a chocolate bar from my hands and heads out after his friends, calling, "Whirr-woo-wuuu . . . whirr-woo-wuuu." Moments later we hear a shrill reply as he disappears into the forest.

"Where's that monkey meat you promised?" Innocent asks Theo.

"I can't even get the fire started. Everything's wet, wet."

"What about the others?"

"No gunshots . . . I don't think they caught anything. We may have to eat moon food," Theo says, returning to the blowpipe.

He's referring to the freeze-dried dinners I've brought along, similar to the ones astronauts dine on. We also have plenty of manioc, dried fruit, chocolate bars, a few pounds of lentils, and a bag of rice that we've agreed to use only in emergencies. Back in Boha, Ange convinced me to leave behind all the tinned food I bought in Epena. The cans were too heavy to lug, he said, and besides, "the best hunters come from Boha, so there will be food on the fire every night."

Innocent goes off to fill the water jugs while I busy myself clearing the ground and gathering fronds from tree ferns to sleep on. The campsite looks as if it has been recently used; the British team must have spent a night here. Someone has built a lean-to and a platform to keep bags off the ground, away from the jungle floor, home to the world champions of decomposition.

Innocent returns lugging five gallons of muddy water, and we begin to filter it with a pricey water purification device I bought at the Outdoor Boutique in New York. The product brochure guaranteed that it "will purify 200 gallons of dangerous, filthy water. . . . Wherever you go, your family will have safe water to drink. No more worries." It yields a mere two quarts before one of the seals pops, and its filters are clogged beyond repair. Innocent and I revert to a simpler method, straining the water through a handkerchief. Larvae, worms, tadpoles, spiders, and other dreck quickly fill the cloth in a writhing mass. We add some chlorine to the water, let it sit for a while, and take a tentative sip. It tastes awful, but it will have to do.

Meanwhile Theo has managed to coax the fire alive, and a steady column of smoke is rising into the air. The three of us are exhausted, but our mood soon shifts, tensing as darkness falls. We blow our whistles, signaling to the men from Boha, but the only reply is from a tree hyrax that grunts, groans, and eventually screams. Theo keeps blowing his whistle, wondering aloud if we've been abandoned. "They've tricked us . . . left us to die."

The tree hyrax cranks up another of its eerie calls and is soon joined by a neighbor. Out of time with each other, the two hyraxes cry out, ascending the scale in quarter-notes until they start screaming again. They rest several seconds before starting over. Theo wants to shoot them. "They're giving me the creeps," he says, grabbing his rifle. Sure that he won't find a target, I wish him luck. Hyraxes, or dassies as they're sometimes called, are the only hoofed animals known to climb trees. Being small, about the size of a rabbit, with black fur, they will be impossible to spot at night.

Theo returns within minutes. He no longer cares about the hyraxes. "Forget them," he says. "It's too spooky out there. Evil spirits are around . . . Stand away from the fire and you can hear them."

Rustling sounds come from all directions, and tens of millions of insects and other creatures are croaking and trilling. A few thump and bark, and one animal sounds just like a cow burping.

Innocent tells Theo to relax. "As long as we don't hear the *molimbo*, we're all right."

Years ago, when a village dispute threatened to disrupt community life, the elders would meet to resolve the situation. If they agreed on a culprit, they'd call together all the males of the village. While the men talked, one person appointed by the elders would hide in the jungle and commence the accusatory *molimbo*, an ancient sequence of preternatural sounds.

"The caller was supposed to make the most frightening noises possible," Innocent explains. The bizarre sounds were directed at the accused and wouldn't stop until that person accepted the judgment of the elders. "It could go on for days."

Branches crunch to our left. Theo spins around, one hand on his juju bag, the other on his pistol.

"Miss us?" Gabriel bounds into the light of the campfire.

"Look!" says Raymond, holding out one of the Ziploc baggies I brought along for plant specimens.

I shine the flashlight on a bagful of grubs. "Dinner?" I ask. "Dessert," Ange answers. "Delicious."

Theo, his old self now that the others have returned, rifles through our supplies and pulls out six freeze-dried entrées. The label on each one reads, "Just add one cup of boiling water . . . A feast in a pouch!"

Theo puts the water on to boil, and Raymond fans the flames. Our campfire, a lone beacon in the dark night, attracts hundreds of moths, including one the size of a hummingbird. They fly kamikaze-like into the flames, their wings flaring up like tissue paper as they combust. In view for a mere second or two before carbonizing, they prove impossible to catch.

My feast in a pouch is a meatloaf that tastes like sawdust floating in a sauce of Elmer's glue. Innocent's beef stroganoff smells remarkably like dog food. The men from Boha are too hungry to complain, but Theo gobbles up his chicken dish and licks the foil clean, murmuring, "Très bien."

Gabriel passes out slices of manioc, which has as much flavor as tofu and is as chewy as shoe leather, but I'm the only one who doesn't seem to enjoy this staple of the Congo. Ange thrusts a hand into the bagful of grubs, elbows me, and points to my notebook.

"You should write this recipe down . . . Never wash the grubs. The dirt adds to the flavor . . . Make sure the pan is real hot." He holds the skillet over the fire, waits several seconds, and spits into the pan. When his saliva skitters across it, he smiles. "Pour in a little water or coconut oil, and add the grubs. Stir and sprinkle a little of this." He reaches into his bag and pulls out an old aspirin bottle filled with brown powder. "Don't use much of this, just a pinch or two . . . Keep stirring until the water is gone. Voilà!"

"What did you add?" I ask.

"That's a secret."

Ange serves us each a scoop of grubs on an arum leaf. Gabriel spreads his portion on some manioc, while Raymond simply sucks them up from the leaf. The grubs have a crisp outer shell and a soft, gooey interior with a slightly bitter taste. I bequeath my share of seconds to the others.

Innocent and Theo help me set up the tent, a two-person affair that will have to accommodate three on this expedition. When I practiced erecting the tent in my apartment in New York, it never took longer than five minutes. Tonight, however, after nearly recreating a lost episode of "The Three Stooges," we secure it only after a half-hour of bumbling and head-knocking. Next time we'll pitch it while there's still light. Climbing inside, I promptly rip the tent's bottom, but at least I discover where I left my knife.

Gabriel walks around our new home, shaking his head as he touches the nylon. "No good for storms," he critiques, swearing that he'd never sleep inside such a flimsy thing.

"Too small for me," Raymond says, stretching his arms and spreading his legs. "This is how I sleep."

I wanted to buy a hammock for this trip, like the one that had served me well in Central America, but I couldn't find one suitable for backpacking in the jungle.

"Only the ground is safe and comfortable," Ange insists.

"What about the bugs?"

"Hah, only weak men cry."

"Drivers?" I ask, referring to the menacing ants. Termites are their usual prey, but they'll attack anything and have been known to strip an elephant to the bone in less than a day.

"Mundélés always complain. We don't," Ange says in a huff. Gabriel and Raymond grunt in agreement.

Theo runs a flashlight over the interior of the tent. "Pardon," he says, and grabs a field guide out of my hand. Seconds later loud thumping noises come from the tent. We inspect his work: five harmless leaf-cutting ants lie squished on the nylon.

"Good book," he says, returning *Butterflies of Africa*.

CHAPTER ◆ 22

THE TENT REEKS of three unwashed bodies, sweat-soaked clothing, and socks that have sprung mushrooms overnight. The insides of my forearms have been tattooed by skin borers, leaving thin red lines like a map of an interstate highway system, and wheals from insect bites dot my legs. The early morning air is as hot and sticky as a dog's breath, and as I sit up, the tent fabric peels away from my skin with a sucking noise.

On the other side of the mosquito netting our guides are sprawled on the ground. Raymond lies spread-eagled, his shirt over his shaven head, dewdrops beaded on his chest hair. Ange is partially buried under leaves stripped from the roof of the lean-to; his left hand clutches his juju bag.

I step out into sapphire light filtering through the dense fog hanging in the forest canopy. As the sun rises, the mist gradually thins, and the bluish light turns into golden green. Dawn arrives and rousts the diurnal animals.

"Who-wuuuuu," a mona monkey calls from its perch three trees away. It bolts the moment I swing in its direction.

I go on a short walk to collect plants and insects and return to find five grumpy men drinking bitter-tasting instant coffee. No one has slept well. Raymond developed a loud cough around midnight that kept animals away and us awake for hours. Theo says he dreamed of ants, which explains why he can't stop scratching himself. Our supply of sugar melted during the night, its Ziploc seal left open after someone's late-night snack. Everything else, including the ever-essential chocolate bars and cigarettes, is intact in triple-ply plastic bags.

We plan an easy day of walking. The edge of the swamp abutting Lake Télé, where we'll make camp, is less than five hours away. This will leave most of the afternoon for hunting, and Ange doesn't want to waste a minute of it.

"Today, one monkey for every one of my toes . . . Tokay." He bounds to his feet, emptying his coffee cup on the fire. The steam rises into our faces.

I ask Ange to wait a few minutes. There's only one beetle left to catalogue from my morning stroll. Innocent translates his response, my first exposure to Lingala profanity. Raymond adjusts the dressing on his thigh wound, which I've been treating since before we left, and steps between me and Ange. Again he agrees to shepherd me and Innocent, and our expedition divides into two parties. Gabriel promises to leave conspicuous trail markers and, together with Ange and Theo, he jogs northward, leaving us to clean up camp and follow at our own pace.

The birds are crooning on high, but I can't see any of them through the lush greenery. Parrots whistle and caw with touracos, as red-bellied flycatchers add silvery bars between the "shoo-wees" of sooty bulbuls. A warbler's lilting song is nearly lost in the ringing cries of a yellow-crowned bishop, while several chestnut wattle-eyes crackle and croak. Raymond shrugs his shoulders in answer to each of my questions about the avian world. He has never given birds a second thought; there's not enough meat on them to interest him.

"Pygmies know birds, not Boha men," he says, picking up a branch and pretending it's a blowgun, the weapon of choice among bird hunters. "Crossbows are too loud, and shotguns turn a bird into feathers."

His grandfather knew how to use a blowgun, but Raymond has tried only a few times. His specialty is game he can strike with a spear. "Listen," he says, and treats us to a rendition of several mammalian calls; his impersonation of a leopard's cough is frighteningly good.

Innocent and I are hunched over a silver-gray beetle the size of a walnut, when Raymond spins and snatches up his spear. Several branches crash down from the canopy. Overhead we see a troop of red colobus monkeys scampering past. This thumbless species with a long, slender tail rarely ventures far from home base. They're out of range, so Raymond can only sit back with us and watch the brazen parade.

Ange, Theo, and Gabriel all greased their rifles before they left. Might the monkeys have smelled the freshly oiled weapons and kept their distance until they were sure no guns were around? Raymond says a hunter's success has nothing to do with when the shotguns are oiled. "When the gun spirits say no, it is no. Sometimes you see monkeys, sometimes you don't."

I ask if rubbing a leaf on a gun to soothe its spirit has a practical purpose as well, such as masking the odor of oil.

"You don't understand," Raymond lectures. "The tree spirit talks to the gun spirit for the human spirit . . . It has nothing to do with oil or leaves. Spirits, mundélé, spirits. They do everything."

I count eighteen monkeys in this troop. In the lead and at

the rear are two old males with long wisps of gray fringing their otherwise reddish cheeks. The dominant male travels in the middle of the harem and hustles the females along whenever they dawdle. There's one other male who has no set position in the troop, most likely a youngster who will one day either dethrone the leader or be exiled from the tribe. Red colobuses are the acrobats of the jungle, and these swing through the lianas with spectacular speed and grace.

▼

"The bad boy," Raymond says, pointing to a dark form trailing the troop. It stays well behind the others, never closing the gap. As it nears, I can see that it is a black-and-white colobus, heftier than its red-furred cousins, with a gray Amish beard and long white hair sprouting from its sides.

While the troop of reds moves through the area and disappears, the black-and-white lingers on a branch directly above the tent, watching us break camp. I leave a handful of dried fruit for him as we set off.

After hiking several kilometers, we find a barwood tree encased by a strangler dotted with orchids; the vine spirals up the trunk like a stairway in a lighthouse. It seems sturdy enough to climb, I think, tugging and feeling for handholds. I've been collecting bulbs and cuttings from ground plants, and this seems like a good way to pick up a few orchids. I climb the first ten feet easily, and only a little bit higher is the first of several splendid epiphytes; just above them, astonishingly, is what appears to be a bromeliad. While thousands of bromeliads are found in Central and South America, only one species is known to be indigenous to West Africa. I could be on the verge of discovering the second native African bromeliad. A few steps higher, almost within reach of the first orchid, I touch something crinkly and dry. It's sloughed-off snake skin, and from its size I reckon it came from a green mamba.

The bottom orchid is flowering. Its fluted petals, the color of alabaster flecked with cinnabar, harbor golden stamens ringing a delicate pistil dripping with nectar. I run my finger around the carpel and am immediately beseiged by red ants pouring out from under the orchid. A dozen of them dig their pincers deep into my forefinger, and scores of others race up my arm and attack my neck. I quickly climb back down. The bromeliad remains undisturbed.

"Stand still," Innocent urges, helping brush off the ants. "Use the climbing rope next time."

The bites on my hands and arms are a stinging example of the many symbiotic relationships among species in the jungle. In this case the orchid produces enzymes and other basic foodstuffs that the ants need to subsist; in return, the ants zealously guard the orchid from intruders, save a select beetle species that carries pollen from plant to plant. Without the ants, the orchids would probably become extinct, and without the orchids, the ants would have to find a new food source or die.

As we continue toward the great swamp, I recall how Alain and Gaspar described animism as the sum of all parts in nature, a mosaic, with each piece integral to the overall design. The witch doctor in Boha believed the essence of everything to be the same; what differentiated things, he said, was the power of the spirit imbuing each bit of creation. There's a hierarchy all around us, with man at the top of the worldly order and the gods forming their own astral ranks above man. When I spoke of Mokele-Mbembe as a stirring deep inside the individual, the witch doctor corrected me. Mokele-Mbembe is a god, he explained, and therefore separate from man. "We are this," the witch doctor said, pinching his skin, "and Mokele-Mbembe is that," he added, opening his arms wide and raising his head to the sky. To him, Mokele-Mbembe, along with the other great spirits in the animist pantheon, helped him to understand why coconuts grow on trees and how stars stay in the sky.

"Beesch! . . . beesch!" Innocent calls off to my left. He

points to a branch in a false nutmeg tree, where a lone black-and-white colobus monkey stares down at us. Innocent and Raymond are positive that it's the same one we spotted back at the camp.

Raymond studies the monkey through the binoculars. "He's a messenger," Raymond pronounces, correcting his earlier charge that the monkey was "a bad boy." Innocent agrees: "Messenger, no doubt about it." Raymond slices off a portion of manioc for it. In Ubangi folklore, monkeys often run errands for the gods. If this were a chimpanzee or a gorilla, Raymond would have left an entire loaf of manioc. Gorillas are the guardians of the gods, bouncers protecting their jungle lairs. Chimps are sentries, chattering warnings of danger. When chimps or gorillas appear, it's a sure sign that a powerful spirit is nearby; when a monkey identified as a messenger appears, it means a god is planning his arrival. Raymond tells us to move on: "Let the messenger eat."

I check the map, and by my reckoning we're entering the geographical center of all recorded Mokele-Mbembe sightings. In 1913 a Prussian military commander, Freiherr Von Stein, encountered traces of Mokele-Mbembe the same distance ahead of us as Djéké is behind. He was leading an expedition south from Cameroons, then a German colony, and while exploring the Sangha River, he came across "a monstrous" path in the jungle leading to a molombo vine. His guides recognized the path and droppings as those of Mokele-Mbembe. They told Von Stein about the creature, the biggest animal in the jungle, larger than an elephant and equipped with a long, flexible neck. Other tales of a jungle beast filtered down to Brazzaville, where enterprising journalists wrote dispatches about giant brontos trampling native villages. Six years after Von Stein's expedition, the Smithsonian Institution offered a three-million-dollar reward for one of these Congo dinosaurs, dead or alive. Among those attracted by the bounty was the Englishman Leicester Stevens. He set off accompanied by his dog, Laddie, which had been decorated by the British Army for service as a "barrage dog," or front-line courier during World War I. Stevens told reporters seeing him off that Laddie could take on anything, "from a tank to a dinosaur." Stevens was never heard from again, and natives insisted that he and Laddie were both eaten by Mokele-Mbembe. The Smithsonian later retracted its bounty, and the hunt for the congo dinosaur wasn't resumed until Mackal's expedition in 1980.

Innocent and I are walking ahead of Raymond when we see Ange and Gabriel in the distance and alter course to join them.

Whoosh! A spear whizzes over my shoulder and sticks into a tree. The shaft vibrates on impact, strumming the air: *a-wanngg.*

"Stop!" Raymond shouts.

I stand rooted to the ground, with Innocent trembling next to me. Raymond trots past us to retrieve his spear, yanks it out of the bark, and kisses the tip. He turns and points behind us. "That way."

"You could have hit him," Innocent reprimands Raymond.

"At that distance I don't miss . . . I was aiming at the tree."

He had thrown his spear to stop us from trespassing into the old village grounds of Boha, which are sacrosanct. While it would be bad enough for Innocent to step on a grave, it would be an unspeakable blasphemy for a mundélé to do so.

Raymond leads us off in the opposite direction, and we soon find Theo eating in a roofless lean-to. "We got here two hours ago," Theo says. "We saw a reedbuck. Real big . . . We almost got it, but it escaped into the swamp." After the chase, Ange ordered Theo not to leave the campsite. "He and Gabriel said they had to do something alone."

Raymond pulls out a sharpening stone to hone his spear tip, and tells us to prepare for hunting. Innocent and I scout around for pebbles to use in my slingshot but soon give up, realizing that all surface rocks probably dissolved thousands of years ago.

"If the water and tree roots didn't get them, the acids did," Innocent says, dipping a strip of litmus paper from his kit into a puddle. The paper turns bright red, reacting to the tannic and humic acids leaching from the trees.

The jungle compensates for its lack of minerals through hydrolysis, energy conservation, and efficient recycling. There's no waste here. All organic matter is eventually broken down into usable compounds: rotting leaves nourish bacteria, which in turn fuel protozoans, algae, fungi, termites, ants, millipedes, beetles, centipedes, birds, reptiles, and mammals. Parasites tap the strong for the eventual benefit of countless microscopic organisms. Death begets life.

Because of the jungle's near-constant rainfall, water carries away soil before it has time to accumulate. The topsoil in the rain forest rarely exceeds a foot or two in depth, and when Innocent digs a test hole, he hits clay about sixteen inches down, intimating that the trees around us are less a product of the soil than the soil is a product of the trees. The trees have adapted by evolving buttresses, giant horizontal braces that stabilize vertical growth. This frees the roots from anchor duty, allowing them to grow close to the surface, fanning out in the thin layer of nutrient-rich humus.

Cut down the trees and everything quickly falls out of balance. Erosion accelerates, acidity increases, and nutrients are leached away, not to be replenished naturally through leaf fall and animal excrement. The manioc field in Boha, for instance, is only three years old, but its productivity is almost gone. Raymond told us that the village council plans to slash and burn another chunk of the jungle next year.

When Ange and Gabriel return to the campsite, they pass out limes. "The old trees still work," Gabriel says, slicing open a fruit and sucking the juice. "The spirits will never leave old Boha."

They have been paying their respects to the home of their ancestors. Seventy-three years ago, two missionaries visited old Boha for a day and then disappeared on their way back to Epena. Neither their bodies nor their canoes were ever found, so French investigators summarily concluded that the priests were murdered.

"All lies. Our ancestors were peaceful people," Ange insists.

French troops were sent to exact justice in the colonial manner, killing fifty natives for every dead Frenchman. More than half of the village was massacred, including the chief, his wives, and all his children over the age of seven. The survivors were forced to resettle by the Bai River, where it would be easier for the French to monitor them. The old village was burned to the ground.

"The first mundélés to see Boha were priests, and the next to come were Légionnaires with guns and torches . . . A good introduction to mundélés, eh?" Ange scowls.

CHAPTER ◆ 23

C HASSE!" ANGE SOUNDS the beginning of the hunt.
Our little safari group has obviously not been out-
fitted by Eddie Bauer or Banana Republic. Raymond has no left
sleeve; Gabriel's back pockets are back at home. "Good pot-
holders," he explains. Ange and I have sewed the inside seams
of our pants with philodendron, or tie-tie, as the vine is commonly called.

Gabriel gives us a short reminder in hunting techniques,
telling us to walk on our toes and crouching to demonstrate
how a low center of gravity makes it easier to jump, turn, and
sprint. "Stay low. Stay ready."

"And stay alert for snakes," Ange cautions.

The equatorial rain forest has the highest concentration on
earth of venomous snakes. Some live in the trees and others
on the ground; most are four to seven feet long, with a few

growing to twenty feet. The black mamba is perhaps the most dangerous: two drops of its venom can kill a person. While stories about its speed have been greatly exaggerated (mambas cannot outrace a man), it has unusually quick reflexes and a bellicose nature.

Two varieties of black snake, the burrowing cobra and the African garter snake, live on the ground here, but they are sluggish and shy and rarely bite unless someone unwittingly sits on their shallow burrows. Their relatives in the trees, the Gold's cobra and the black tree cobra, have a tendency to snooze on low branches, from which they can easily fall onto a shoulder or leg. The Gaboon viper is called the "sudden death snake," and its two-and-a-half-inch fangs can pierce a shoe and splinter bone.

"Is the snake bite kit handy?" Innocent asks. I pat the side of my bag. My doctor in New York, bless him, prepared me well for this trip. He's a tropical-disease expert who spent years practicing in West Africa. In the stack of prescriptions he handed me was one for morphine. "Snake serums often don't work, and there's no serum for some snakes . . . Use the morphine if things look bleak. At least you'll go out smiling."

Like the Epena crocodile hunters, the men of Boha coordinate the hunt through hand signals. An open palm means halt; a closed fist means retreat. When Ange, walking about thirty yards ahead, stops suddenly and holds up an open palm, we freeze and concentrate on the myriad jungle sounds. The only unusual thing I detect is the rapid pulse of my heart.

Ange crawls back and whispers, "Dinner." Like a sandlot quarterback, he draws lines of attack on the ground. Everyone but me is assigned a position. Gabriel kindly suggests that I tag along with him.

"We will wait five minutes . . . Move on my whistle," Ange instructs Raymond, who slinks off to circle behind a troop of monkeys. Theo positions himself on the spot; Ange and Innocent head to the left, while I follow Gabriel off to the right.

In the old days, before they had access to guns, villagers used to hunt monkeys with crossbows. "That was hard," Gabriel says. "Men like my grandfather used to hunt duiker and reedbuck with nets," a technique still used by the Pygmies. Made out of vines, usually philodendron or vanilla bean, the nets would be strung from tree to tree. Several men would bury themselves in leaves near the traps, ready to spring on a snared animal with clubs or spears. The rest of the hunting party would spread out in a crescent about a kilometer away and chase the game toward the camouflaged nets. "Today we're much smarter," Gabriel assures me.

A few minutes later Ange mimics the song of a black chat, a repetitious sequence of two notes, and Raymond starts running and shouting, trying to scare the troop our way. The forest erupts with howls and screeches as the older males sound the alert. Birds fly out of the canopy, adding their voices to the tumult. Gabriel sights down his gun barrel at a large crested mangabey in a troop of sixteen crashing through the upper limbs. Several monkeys in the middle of the pack appear clumsy and not particularly frightened; a few even pause to look back at Raymond, who is closing fast.

Gabriel rubs a lucky leaf on his gun sight and keeps the muzzle trained on the large male; he won't fire, though, until Ange, the huntmaster, shoots. He clenches a spare shell between his teeth and blinks rapidly. Sweat beads up on the back of his neck.

Ange fires and Gabriel almost simultaneously pulls his trigger. Blam! The sulfur fumes sting my nostrils. Blam! Gabriel's second shot peppers a tree trunk. Ange fires his second round on the run, and Theo empties half a clip from his automatic. The unwounded mangabeys scramble in terror, leaping out of sight.

Four monkeys have tumbled to the ground, but only one lies motionless. The others careen off in different directions. Raymond calls for help and I race after him, zigzagging in pursuit of a monkey hit in the shoulder; its right arm hangs limp, but it somehow manages to maintain speed.

"Hoy-bah!" Raymond snorts, cocking his arm and loosing the spear without breaking stride. It strikes the ground inches from the mangabey, which cuts left.

"Bad move, Mister Monkey." Raymond grabs the spear and continues the chase. "You should go for the swamp."

This time the spear pierces the mangabey's throat. The monkey falls to the ground, blood gushing out, and in a few seconds is lifeless. Raymond casually puts his foot on the toddler-sized creature and extracts the spear. He picks up the prize by its hand and drags it along. There's no sign of Gabriel and Roland, but we can see Ange and Innocent chasing another mangabey. Ange has his machete out.

"Must save shells," Raymond says. "I've finished off monkeys with my bare hands."

Raymond strings the catch from a sapling, and we backtrack for the one that fell dead; bees, leather beetles, and blowflies are already swarming over it. Carolus Linnaeus, father of taxonomy, called blowflies the most voracious creatures on earth after watching them strip a horse faster than a pride of lions could. Raymond lifts the dead monkey and smacks it repeatedly against the ground, scattering the insects.

"This will be delicious," he promises.

Innocent and Ange return with their prize in two pieces, Ange carrying a body and Innocent a head wrapped in an arum leaf. Gabriel and Roland show up empty-handed. "He went into the swamp, and we lost," Gabriel explains.

Innocent checks to see that all the mangabeys are males. There are heavy fines for killing a female.

"Brazzaville doesn't have to tell us about the jungle," Ange snaps at Innocent. "What about the finger sellers. They're the ones."

Traders in Kinshasa sell gorilla fingers, hands, and internal organs, which are coveted by the Chinese and Koreans for their supposed curative powers. Marin, my black-market contact, assured me that genuine shrunken heads and gorilla parts were available in Zaire, but he refused to take me to these benighted traders, sure that they would kill us if we didn't buy anything. A shrunken head, he told me, goes for five hundred dollars, and a gorilla finger costs fifty dollars.

"The state doesn't understand the jungle," Ange adds. "Ask our cousins and comrades in Ouesso. You're wrong if you think they want their forest cut . . ."

Innocent slightly bows his head. I sense that he agrees with Ange about the deforestation around Ouesso, but his loyalty lies with the Forestry Department, right or wrong.

The gunshots and commotion have scared off everything worth eating except snakes, which are deaf, though they can sense vibrations traveling through the air and ground. Raymond heads back out to hunt them as we turn toward camp.

Pulling out my butterfly net, I trap and release a long-tailed Congo swallowtail and an assortment of whites and blues, all of them common species already in my collection. But under a false nutmeg tree, fluttering between two buttresses, is a handsome butterfly I don't have, a dusky swordtail. It's an agile flier and leads me on a dizzying course, and I hoot triumphantly once it's captured. Only a few collections have this rare black butterfly spangled with emeralds; a connoisseur might pay five hundred dollars or more for this specimen. I study its long, slender tail and gaze appreciatively at the row of green disks running down the middle of its wings, each oval precisely drawn and a bit larger than the one below it. There are delicate splashes of light green in the subapical area, and faint stripes along its costa tease the eye. Carefully pinching its thorax and opening the killing jar, I take one last look at the living butterfly. There has been enough killing for one day, I decide, opening my fingers and releasing the swordtail.

Raymond returns without any snakes, but he has found several fallen birds' nests and a large chunk of *vaka*, hardened tree resin, all of which make excellent tinder. Ange has sharpened his machete and stands poised like a sacrificial priest — palms together in a prayerful manner, eyes shut, the machete tucked under an arm. Gabriel lays the gutted monkeys out on a log, and Ange mutters something that makes the others bow their heads. He lifts the machete and grunts mightily as the blade comes down; three whacks later, the first carcass is split into two pieces and Ange lines up the next one. Gabriel uses his hands to disembowel and salt the raw flesh.

Flames vault into the sky, their tips dancing above our heads as Raymond and Theo both fan the coals. Gabriel surveys their work with a critical eye and points to an area that isn't hot enough. "Make it grow," he shouts.

Once the fire is to his liking, Gabriel lobs the meat into the blaze, and a horrid smell of burning flesh and hair gags me. Innocent holds his nostrils, but the others inhale the smoke as if it's precious incense. Gabriel waves everyone back. He's cooking tonight and doesn't want any interference. He uses his machete like a spatula to spread the salt and tend the meat. The body fat dripping into the flames sizzles and pops; the monkey skin tightens, and the body parts look more and more human. Grease spits at us, and Raymond sucks the oily stains out of his shirt. Gabriel flips the meat after a few minutes. More than five minutes a side is too much, I'm told. "You want it chewy," Gabriel says.

He lifts the cooked meat onto a bed of arum leaves, where Ange quarters it and hands us each a piece. The meat has been blistered to charcoal on the outside, but it's pink, bloody, and nearly raw on the inside. I throw my piece back on the fire until it's well done. It has a gamy, sour taste, but I manage to eat most of a thigh.

That night around three, a fierce gust of wind startles us awake. Thunderclaps echo in the distance. Ange, Gabriel, and Raymond stagger out from under the lean-to and shine their flashlights up into the canopy. The trees are gyrating wildly, shaking leaves, nests, and twigs to the ground. Innocent and Theo jump up, but I stay inside the tent, comfortably wrapped in my sheet.

Gusts give way to a steady blow that rips into the forest, bending branches and whipping saplings back and forth. Then an ominous lull descends. At sea, in tropical waters, a stillness like this presages gale-force winds, with a five- to ten-minute interlude before squalls buffet the area. Aboard ship I'd drop the sails, set the drogue, and dash below, life jacket on, praying for dear life. In the jungle I stare out happily, feeling safe inside the tent, eager for the big show to begin.

The rain commences as a thunderclap rattles the earth. Purple-blue flashes lance the jungle blackness, freezing everything in an icy light; millions of volts crackle through the air, zapping limbs and trunks. The wind rages, with gusts over forty knots. A sapling near the tent bends to the jungle floor. Everyone but me is outside, their heads thrown back and their flashlights slicing through the downpour. They move back and forth in unison, as if dancing. More lightning forks down, and I can see Innocent waving to me. The wind sweeps his voice away.

Kaboom! A tree falls somewhere close by, sending tremors through the ground and up my body. A heavy branch tears through the tent roof and takes a chunk out of the ground near my foot. I jump outside, joining the others and quickly learn the dance: dodge the falling debris and duck under the whip-lashing lianas. A tent is no haven in a jungle squall.

My feet are raw by the time the storm passes, twenty minutes later. Soaked to the bone and exhausted, we crawl into a heap under the lean-to. I sleep next to Gabriel, who recaps tonight's lesson in jungle survival: "If you can't see it coming, you won't know where to run."

I expect to awaken to a devastated landscape, with uprooted trees and ravaged undergrowth, but surprisingly, the rain forest is relatively unscathed, proving its resiliency in the worst weather. The diversity of trees and their flexibility, as well as the stabilizing effect of all the interconnected lianas, protected the forest from severe damage. Gabriel says these storms hit the area every couple of months or so, with the most violent ones coming at the beginning of the rainy season, which officially starts this week. "We don't have glass in our windows at home, we have shutters."

It's sour coffee and soggy cookies for Innocent and me while the others happily gnaw monkey for breakfast. The great swamp is only a mile away, so we break camp early, expecting to reach Lake Télé by midafternoon. We haven't seen our friend, the black-and-white colobus monkey, and I doubt it's anywhere around after the hunt and last night's storm. Even so, Innocent and Raymond leave out some dried fruit. To neglect the messenger, Raymond says, is to insult the god who employs him.

The leaf clutter gradually gives way to soft, moss-covered ground. Saprophytes dot the area, rising from the earth like so many lingams painted in Shiva's favorite colors of red, pink, and purple. Occasionally one of them will ejaculate its spores in a small cloud, making our eyes tear and setting Raymond to sneezing, mighty blasts that carry spittle yards downwind. As the jungle floor grows squishier, new flora appears: mangroves, tree ferns, and cycads. Instead of arum and maranta plants, there are now many different species of ferns, and great strings of moss replace the woody lianas we've been accustomed to seeing.

Gabriel grabs my arm and steers me away from a small muddy pool that smells of sulfur. "Devil," he cautions. "That's his mouth . . . His stomach has no bottom. Watch out, they eat men."

Gingerly, I dip a finger into the black goo. One taste tells me that it's oil, and an unsavory image of oil rigs and pipelines looms before me.

Soon we're slogging through ankle-deep water. The air reeks of methane, the stench increasing as the brown, scum-covered water deepens. Most of the trees are denuded, broken-limbed, and leaning at odd angles, as if blown over in an atomic blast. The sky is open above us, but the sun is blotted out by a heavy ground mist that leaves an acrid taste in my mouth. Hundreds of dragonflies skim the water, darting left, then right, their iridescent red and green bodies conspicuous in this bleak, postnuclear landscape. When they land on the black fungi girdling the dead trees, they look like jeweled brooches on velvet. Mosquitoes, newly hatched and hungry, buzz around. Tadpoles, salamanders, and frogs dive and hop as we pass, only to pop back up seconds later, blinking madly. Water spiders skitter on the waves we make, floating on their buoyant leg hairs. A loud splash off to our right sends us all racing onto the nearest fallen tree trunk, where we stand searching for the ripples of a swimming snake or crocodile. Raymond drops into a crouch as Gabriel and Ange load their shotguns and Theo flicks off the safety on his AK-47. Innocent and I strike the water with sticks, trying to attract whatever made the sound, but nothing appears. Even so, we wait for several minutes; there's no serum for the bite of an African water cobra.

A bird flies overhead, and for a moment it looks to be a member of the pterosaur family, a *Quetzalcoatlus* to be exact, last thought to have flown in the late Cretaceous period. Focusing my camera, zooming in and out on the bird's coal-black leathery wings, I realize that's it's only a cormorant.

The guns remain loaded, safeties off, as we slosh on through the swamp. We walk cautiously, our eyes fixed on the scummy surface. Any splashing sound brings us to a stop. "Shhh!" Gabriel says every time, scanning the murk. Sometimes we sink up to our ankles in mud and it's a struggle to pull free. Skin borers by the hundreds tunnel through my arms and hands. Another type of borer is digging through the soles of my feet. These worms begin life no larger than a match head, but given the right conditions, they can grow to the size of a small snake within the leg, their growth arrested only by knee joints and ligaments. Eventually they eat through the calf and exit from the skin just below the knee.

Gradually the water level falls, and we sight a green tree line through the fog. A salamander wiggles by and I scoop it up, depositing it a few inches beyond the lip of Mokele-Mbembe's home turf, a land stalled in time.

We leave the swamp behind and reenter the rain forest, where flora blossoms and sweet smells emerge. Sunshine pours through openings in the canopy, and for the first time in days, we have shadows. The others bend down to touch their silhouettes, and I do the same. In animist doctrine, shadows are manifestations of the soul, which leave the body's side at night to roam the spirit world and gather dreams.

"No one's shadow is the same," Innocent says. "When we don't see them for a while, we worry. They protect us," he adds, explaining that witch doctors often cast their spells at night, when the body, unguarded by its shadow, is most susceptible to devils.

We take a break under a giant plane tree to scrape the mud off our clothes. The great swamp turned out to be neither great nor perilous. It was only a few miles wide, and the most dangerous creature we encountered was a poisonous frog, a killer only if you somehow manage to eat two of them at a sitting.

CHAPTER 24

Vasco de Balboa first sighted the Pacific Ocean from the height of a tree, but I spot Lake Télé from the mud, spreadeagled after tripping over a root. Unexpectedly able to see beneath the shrub layer, I glimpse a broad, vague expanse shimmering in the distance.

Leaping to my feet with excitement, I urge the others to pick up the pace, but Ange grabs my shoulder bag and holds me back. We're guests, he explains, and we're expected to honor Mokele-Mbembe with certain rituals. There are prayers to be said and an offering to be made. The men from Boha, each a priest in the service of Mokele-Mbembe, must lead the way; otherwise we risk angering the beast and bringing a damaging curse upon ourselves. In the past they've let the outsiders forge ahead, secretly hoping they'd suffer the repercussions.

"We need food, so we do it right this time," Ange declares. "Touch the water before we do, and it will be the last drink you ever take."

We dump our gear at the campsite and walk several yards to the shore. Innocent, Theo, and I stand back as the three men drop to their knees and pray. Afterward they sip the water, splash some on their chests, and invite us to do the same. Gabriel makes a small raft from sticks, and Ange pulls out a piece of manioc and two limes and places them on the raft. I add my own tribute of dinosaur-shaped cookies brought especially from America.

Being the tallest, I'm asked to push the raft beyond the snags. As I wade into the water, Ange asks Mokele-Mbembe to tolerate our presence and to bless us with a plentiful supply of food. When the water starts lapping my chest, I give the raft a gentle shove.

Feeling comfortable in the lukewarm water, I decide to float awhile and contemplate the lake surroundings. Congolese myth refers to Télé as the inner sanctum of the god-beast, its water a fount blessed by the god himself. Perhaps Mokele-Mbembe is observing me right now. The lake is bordered by thirteen sheltered inlets, or lobes, each one big enough to conceal a family of twenty-ton dinosaurs. Every inlet leads to a stream. A few of them feed the swamp; one flows to the Bai River, twenty kilometers to the west; and others trickle in from the forest, connecting Télé to a network of satellite lakes. Raymond says that Mokele-Mbembe travels along these streams, as its body is too large for it to traverse the gnarled jungle.

"This is his home," Raymond said, "but he goes anywhere water goes."

I look for molombo vines, which reportedly bear the god's favorite food. The molombo fruits that I've seen on the trail were the size of softballs, with the texture of an unripe pear;

they had a sour taste and oozed a milky latex. The shoreline is crowded with cycads and tree ferns, which botanists often refer to as "living fossils" because they've hardly changed in hundreds of millions of years. Cycads range from only two feet tall to over forty feet. Unisexual, with primitive reproductive systems, they all have thick stems crowned by pinnate leaves. Wherever coal beds are found today, cycads once flourished.

"Climb aboard," Raymond calls from the stern of a leaky pirogue. Innocent sits forward, bailing with a cook pot. I'm content to stay in the water. There will be plenty of time to row around the lake.

"Crocodiles live here," Raymond warns. I wave him off. I'm only twenty-five yards from shore, and besides, Rothermel assured me that only vegetarian species of crocodile lived in the lake.

"The biggest one I ever caught was over there, next to that fallen tree," Raymond says, pointing to a spot on the eastern shore. "It was five meters long. Teacher measured the skin for me." I swim to the pirogue; only man-eating Nile crocodiles grow that big.

Raymond poles us along with his spear. Two pirogues are kept moored at the campsite, and this eleven-footer, with its punked bow and cracked keel, is the better of the pair. Both were adzed years ago, when Raymond was a young boy, and it's doubtful they will be replaced soon. He toes the paddle floating in the bilge and groans, "It takes days to make one of these . . . The next time you come, bring a boat from America. None of us wants to make a new pirogue."

The water in Lake Télé is a dark sherry color, but its taste would dismay any vintner, being highly acidic, with a tongue-numbing amount of tannin. Several dozen species of fish inhabit the lake, and Raymond says some of the perch weigh more than ten kilos. Catfish are his favorite, though, and he boasts of one he speared that weighed more than 120 pounds.

Oddly, my field guides don't mention any fish of that size in West Africa.

"Do your books talk about dinosaurs?" Innocent asks.

Gun blasts boom from the other side of the lake, where our companions are hunting, and we see a tree limb shake. "Très bien," Raymond whispers and smacks his lips.

Above us, peering through a thin shield of mangrove leaves, a half-dozen monkeys watch the canoes. They're diademed guenons, named for their crown of projecting forehead hair and overgrown eyebrows. Near them is a troop of green monkeys, easily identified by the males' lurid blue scrotums. A few are pulling at leaves, and others are grabbing for insects. Their expandable cheek pouches are stuffed with food, making them look as if they have mumps.

The next series of gunshots sends them scampering for cover but has no discernible effect on the male cicadas, which keep singing their monotonous love songs. Until they find a mate, they won't shut up. Jean-Henri Fabre, the French entomologist and author of *The Social Life of Insects*, once demonstrated their resolve. He enlisted the help of the army to set up a field gun under a tree infested with cicadas. Two rounds were fired, but the unfazed cicadas kept on singing.

Raymond turns the boat around, and the bow of the double-ended canoe becomes the stern. As I start paddling, Innocent points out a forest hog about seventy yards away on the eastern shore. Barrel-shaped and covered in bristly auburn hair, it must weigh three hundred pounds. Forest hogs have razor-sharp tusks, and in Boha I heard of a villager who was gored in the thigh by one and died from gangrene. The hog is fiercely rooting for something, and even though we're upwind, within range of its sensitive nose, it doesn't seem to have noticed us. Having learned my lessons well from Alain and Gaspar, I feather the paddle at the end of each stroke and make sure the blade reenters the water at a steep angle, slicing the surface, not punching it. We glide silently along.

Raymond kisses the tip of his spear and assumes his stance, right arm cocked, ready to fire. We're forty yards away when the hog thrusts its snout into the air, grunts twice, and reels into the jungle, flattening shrubs and gaining speed as it goes. Raymond throws his spear and misses the hog by less than a foot. He smiles though, pleased that he got this close. No one from Boha has ever speared a hog from a boat; usually a kill comes only after a long, chaotic chase by a half-dozen men and dogs.

Raymond remembers seeing hippos in the lake when he was a boy, but Pygmies and hunters from Boha decimated the population years ago. There may be a few cloistered in the remote small lakes to the north and northwest, but that's Pygmy territory, and men from Boha won't venture there. Jungle elephants are still a common sight on these shores, I'm told, coming and going along regular routes. When I ask about exploring the land of the Pygmies, Raymond starts talking in Lingala, shaking his head and wagging a finger. Innocent translates.

"He says you're crazy . . . That land is taboo. Devils are everywhere . . . Even talking about it is crazy."

Several hundred yards off the starboard rail, we spot an animal the size of a small deer taking a sip of water. It's too far away to identify, but its spindly legs and bluish color suggest a duiker. Unlike the hog, it casts nervous glances in every direction; sighting us, it retreats calmly into a thicket of vines.

Raymond wants to steer across the lake, skipping the northern section. "Only birds over there," he complains. With Innocent's help, I prevail and keep the boat headed for the waterfowl. They don't seem to mind our presence as we drift in for a closer look. Near the shore stands a goliath heron almost five feet tall, with long stick legs and massive grayish wings. Its bill is longer than my forearm. A little farther out is a blue-brown tiger bittern. The species is known to be both jittery and elusive, taking flight at the first inkling of danger, but this particular bird appears unconcerned about the three men in a pirogue; perhaps, for the first time, a bird is enjoying my soft renditions from my avian songbook. Flocks of tree ducks and Hartlaub ducks bob in the deep water and dabble closer to shore. Off to one side, as if shunned by the other fowl, is a gaggle of knob-nosed geese. Their necks and heads are splotched in black, and a large ugly comb resembling a goiter sits atop their bills. To the right, in a snag jutting out into the lake, a nesting dabchick eyes us nervously.

Raymond digs in his spear and impishly thrusts the pirogue toward the birds. The tiger bittern leads the others aloft. The ducks run along the surface, the muffled patter of their webbed feet building as they gain speed. The herons pump their mighty wings and throw out their necks, straining skyward, but once aloft, they make flight look easy.

"Shhh!" Raymond bids. He turns the canoe around and starts flashing instructions with his left hand while he aims the spear with his right hand. I watch the veins in his neck bulge as he cocks his arm again.

"Nice shot!" Innocent says.

With a *twang*, a lizard is nailed to a tree twenty-five yards away. We land, and Raymond jumps ashore to retrieve the two-foot-long reptile. It has a triple-horned snout and a stubby tail, with yellowish skin flecked in black.

"Good eating," Raymond guarantees, "but I want his grand-father." He flings the lizard onto my feet in the bilge. Its legs twitch, and I jump backward, nearly capsizing us.

Two years ago he speared a twelve-foot lizard with the same coloring on the western shore. "It was longer than the pirogue," Raymond says. I roll my eyes in disbelief — not even monitor lizards grow that large. He opens his juju bag to show me one of its horns, about the size of my thumb. Could it have been a small chipekwe?

"No . . . no," he repeats. A chipekwe horn wouldn't fit inside his bag. According to Raymond, they are indeed twenty-five to thirty feet long. "Chipekwes are big and powerful gods . . . I could never kill one. The spirit would speak to me here and here," he says, pointing to his right temple and his heart.

Raymond doesn't embellish his stories about giant creatures. He neither talks about nor believes in fire-breathing beasts and animals that can disappear into thin air. "I just say what I saw and what I know," he claims. Innocent confides to me that he believes Raymond's accounts of record-sized fish and animals, but I haven't made up my mind, still anxious to see evidence of the monster menagerie.

There's no one at the camp when we return. Raymond buries the lizard under a mound of leaves and takes off to look for snakes, leaving me and Innocent to set up the campsite. Previous expeditions have left us three lean-tos and several raised platforms. Bits of aluminum foil lie crumpled in the ashes of a campfire pit, and gobs of plastic hang from the sides of two semi-charred logs. Someone has made racks for drying clothes and hanging bags. After adding our initials to those of the Brits carved in a nearby tree, we reroof the lean-tos and collect fronds for our beds.

In a short time, ants and beetles are swarming over the lizard carcass, and I suggest we build a food locker, one we can hoist into the air. I sketch a design for a cage with a latching side panel, but an hour later, when we string it from a tree, it looks more like a medieval torture device.

"No more design projects for you," Innocent declares.

Nimbostratus clouds, greasy black and wet looking, start rolling in from the west. Squeezed under them is a menacing wall of battleship gray streaked with lightning. Soon day becomes night and rain pours down.

During the next two days, we see more rain than a Bedouin might experience in a lifetime. The downpour never lets up, but the wind comes and goes, swirling in squalls and then leaving us long stretches of calm. Around the camp tempers flare. It's impossible to keep a fire going, and cold roast monkey is the only item on the menu. Ange and the other hunters periodically go hunting, but return each time empty-handed. Innocent and I search the forest for dinosaur trails and molombo vines, but we, too, come up empty, finding a few vines, but none that bear fruit.

CHAPTER ◆ 25

A FRESH EVENING BREEZE chases away the clouds, and the sky flicks on its lights. The constellation of the Ship floats over the treetops; off its bow and a bit to the east, the Wolf winks at me, and the Crow, with its bill pointed at Sipca, seems ready to steal the virgin's jewel. Moonlight transforms the dull-colored lake water into a silvery ellipse. Everything seems larger in this light; the lake looks to be an inland sea, and the trees are masts of an outsized fleet, the vast armada of Mokele-Mbembe riding at anchor.

Mole crickets emerge from their burrows with a whirring sound; ground crickets stridulate, playing their comblike organs. I time their chirps over a fourteen-second period and add forty to determine the temperature, a trick I learned as a child reading *The Old Farmer's Almanac*. Tonight's results seem accurate, 69 degrees Fahrenheit. A hornbill shouts from the west, and a greater bushbaby punctuates the night with its disturbingly childlike screams. The first Western explorers to hear the call of a bushbaby, thinking it was a lost toddler, went out to help, only to discover a dog-sized animal, with a long bushy tail and a powerful set of lungs. Bushbabies leave messages for one another by depositing varying amounts of urine on a tree limb, and I wonder how much urine it takes to describe six men seated around a campfire.

"Kree . . . kree." An unusually shrill noise is getting closer by the second. Ange and Gabriel stop cleaning the rust off their guns and glance about. As I stand up, a bat zips past my face, and behind it, in hot pursuit, is a bat hawk.

"Kree . . . kree," the hawk skirls, pursuing its prey like a fighter plane.

We catch glimpses of the chase in the moonlight. The bat soars and swerves, changing direction every few seconds, but it can't shake the raptor.

"Kree . . . kree." They head toward us again.

Theo picks up his machete, holding it as if he's a batter at the plate, and swings wildly at the fliers. Crepuscular predator and prey spiral around the campfire until the bat flies into the side of the tent and clings to it. The hawk banks and heads in for the kill, but Innocent waves a stick and shouts, forcing it back over the water.

"Shall we add it to the stew?" Gabriel asks, looking at the fruit bat, and we shake our heads no. He's already stirred in monkey meat, lentils, wild butter beans, water, and half a bottle of scotch.

Ange tosses a slice of lime at the trembling bat, which refuses to move. "Take it, eat," he urges. "Tonight you live; tomorrow . . . who knows?" Turning to look at me, he adds, "Death can come at any moment in the forest, eh?" I muster a smile and nod.

Up well before dawn, invigorated by a cloudless pastel sky

and calm breeze, I launch a pirogue. Taking soundings after every third paddle stroke, I'm unable to find any water deeper than nine feet, and that's near the middle of the lake. Anywhere within a kilometer of the shore, I can touch bottom using the seven-foot-long paddle. Not much water for a large creature to hide under.

As the sun climbs above the horizon, dozens of birds start flying across the water toward the eastern shore. I follow the parade to a pair of fruiting fig vines, where a party of barbets are greedily pecking at the fruit, chattering between bites and whistling as they preen their red chest feathers. A few gray parrots crowd in, hooting and shrieking as they climb over the vines. When the barbets take off, green fruit pigeons and warblers land. More and more birds arrive and depart in waves, with one species displacing another as if they're on a scheduled breakfast plan. By seven-thirty only a few stragglers, mostly forest robins, are left on the two vines.

I arrive back at camp in time for the first pot of coffee. Theo hands me a cup, and to my surprise it tastes better than any we've had on the trip. Lake Télé water is so bitter that I expected the coffee to be barely drinkable.

"Spices," Theo announces proudly. "I've added scotch to the jerry cans . . . Two shots for every liter."

Usually I make my medical rounds after dinner, but working by flashlight has taxed my already marginal skills, so I decide to switch office hours to the morning. Gabriel has a long gash across his right side, the result of a cousin carelessly swinging his machete. When I first looked at it in Boha, maggots were wiggling in the pus, but now a scab is forming. The wound on Raymond's thigh is also healing. Ange, though, has foot trouble that I doubt will go away until he sees a real doctor in Impfondo. We thought we had discovered the source of the pain two days ago when I located and removed a nail-sized splinter near the ball of his left foot; however, the aching persisted, and this morning I understand why. I can see the head of a worm where the splinter had been. Knowing that any segment of the parasite left in his foot will rot and fester, I have to dig most of it out with a scalpel, using only gentle pressure with the tweezers. Ange grits his teeth, yet he assures me that the blade doesn't hurt; he groans only after I show him the extracted worm and tell him that more are likely to emerge.

All in all, we're in good health, except for the diarrhea that plagues each of us. To augment our supply of antidiarrhetics, I've been collecting shavings from the wood of the *Garcinia punctata* to brew a tea. Patrick taught me this curative in the Bronx and predicted that I would learn dozens of other useful herbal remedies from African witch doctors. However, the witch doctor in Boha told me he had not collected plants in years. "Penicillin is better than anything I ever came up with," he observed. He never wrote down the traditional herbal remedies, and "it has been so long that I've forgotten what works on what." Gabriel's favorite medicine is Alka-Seltzer; he loves the bubbles and fizz.

Once the clinic closes, we pair off for the day. Ange and Theo head west to hunt monkey; Raymond and Gabriel go east after snake and hog; Innocent and I climb aboard the pirogue and set off around the lake. We begin our circumnavigation by looking for molombo vines and for wide swaths near the shore. Drifting as much as paddling, we take our time. Innocent tends a fishing line off the stern, using one of my lures, a Rebel Call, a yellow plug the size of a minnow covered in green and pink acrylic hair. When he works the line, pulling it with sudden jerks, the lure looks just like a gaily colored tadpole.

"I'll make a believer of you," he says, assuring me that he'll catch a giant perch today.

We locate and map eight more molombo vines, three laden

with fruit. I examine the ground carefully around each of them, but find no footprints bigger than a mongoose's. Together we clean out the debris and smaller plants around the molombos, to make it easier to read future tracks.

We're back aboard the pirogue when Innocent, looking through the binoculars, says, "Liambas," Lingala for hemp. It was one of the first words I learned in the native tongue, and I start paddling in the direction he's looking. We jump ashore near a fine cluster of cannabis plants basking in a sunny patch near a mangrove. Unfortunately, all of them are stripped of buds, and a few have had branches ripped off. I select handfuls of the smaller, more flavorful leaves and wonder how to dry them in this humid environment.

"Just eat them . . . like him up there," Innocent recommends, nodding toward a male mangabey who lolls in the crook of a tree with the remains of a cannabis branch dangling from one hand, totally uninterested in us.

The next day, after coffee laced with scotch, we decide to explore the inlets and feeder streams, the so-called pathways of Mokele-Mbembe. As we paddle into the first inlet, a half-dozen lily trotters, *Actophilornis africana*, loose one-note staccato calls as they bound from pad to pad and disappear from view. The inlet is so tightly packed with huge lilies that we have to slice through them with a machete to move along. Frogs croak their displeasure as we disrupt their floating kingdoms, and scorpions arch their stingers as we sink their ships. Fish follow in our wake, sucking in the displaced insects. Slowly we work our way into the mouth of the feeder stream, a flattened green oval at the entrance to an arbored tunnel.

The sun-loving lilies thin out, and the going gets easier as we enter the cool shadows of the tunnel-like growth. We ship the paddles and grab the overhead lianas to pull ourselves along. The deeper we go, the quieter it becomes, and eventually we can hear little more than our own heavy breathing.

Within seventy-five yards, we are out of the tunnel and in the jungle.

"What's the name of this stream?" Innocent asks.

I flip through my notebook, looking for the map I drew with the name of each stream as identified by Ange and Raymond. "Here it is . . . Bokoupe Stream."

We tie up the pirogue and walk for several kilometers along the banks of the Bokoupe until the stream narrows and finally disappears under the soggy leaf litter. Innocent thinks the Bokoupe looks like an ideal trail for a dinosaur, but we find no giant footprints or trampled plants. Innocent does, however, find a colossal mound of excrement. I approach it with a skeptical eye and a pinched nose, knowing that similar finds attributed both to Yeti and Nessie have turned out to belong to some opium eater, either animal or human. In the end, Innocent and I agree that this is not dinosaur stool at all, but that of some large ungulate, probably a reedbuck.

Off to our right we hear a loud belching sound and turn to see a goliath frog. As we run after it, the frog turns and threatens us with a doglike "woof," inflating itself to the size of a soccer ball.

"Watch this," Innocent says, booting the frog and sending it flying ten yards through the air. When he was a kid, he explains, neighborhood teams used goliath frogs as footballs.

"Woof," the frog barks, apparently unfazed.

As we sit down to take a break, leaning against the buttress of a plane tree, we hear a sniffling noise. Looking around, I see nothing unusual, but I feel a sharp jab in the rear and jump to my feet, sure I've been bitten by a snake. The snout of a pangolin pokes through the ground near the buttress, its sharp claws gripping the edge of a hole. Leaves must have been covering the opening because I had checked the spot carefully before sitting. Wanting to photograph the armor-plated ant-eater, we try to coax it out in the open, but it disappears back into its hole. Most jungle burrows are shallow affairs, but this one is deep enough to swallow the five-foot stick Innocent uses as a probe.

We continue north, pushing into the uncharted land of the Pygmies. Innocent likens the maps I draw to the electrical diagram that came with his faulty Russian-made stereo system: "lots of lines that looked correct but weren't." We discover a massive termite hill encircled by arum plants, and we put our ears to it, listening to the hum of industry within. There may be up to a quarter-million termites inside the volcano-shaped nest, and to avoid being swarmed, we're careful to cut only a small opening with our knives. Having excavated a dime-sized hole, we watch the blind workers busily repair the breach within minutes. They work like plasterers, using their mandibles as trowels to mix pulp with a paste they secrete through their mouths.

The low-pitched hooting sound of a pygmy rail ominously fills the air. These ground-dwelling birds fly in short hops, and this one sounds as if it's nearby, less than a hundred yards to our left. As I start to track it, Innocent grabs my arm and leads me away. He says pygmy rails are the voices of ghosts who cannot rest in peace; most often they're souls who have been cheated or lied to in an earlier life. Before they can pass serenely into another form, they first must be satisfied with revenge. As the pygmy rail starts up again, Innocent tells me to close my mouth and cover my ears. "Don't let the spirit enter your body."

A half-kilometer farther on we see a small lake in the distance, no doubt one of Télé's satellites. Standing on the western shore are two bay duikers, not much larger than sheep, with short fawn-colored hair and a broad black stripe along their spines. They calmly lap water, each posed with a front leg in the air, bent at the knee. We approach carefully, but something startles them and they gallop off like horses out of a starting gate.

"Get down," Innocent cautions a few moments later. He falls to the ground and pulls me with him. "There . . . at the other end of the lake."

A leopard slinks into view. No wonder the duikers ran. It yawns, and I can see its teeth and pink tongue through the binoculars. The cat approaches the water casually, stretches out, and takes a drink, its front paws sinking into the mud.

"All alone forever," Innocent whispers and tells me a Fang folk tale. Long ago a leopard fell into a pit and was pulled out by a turtle, which the leopard promptly ate. Its stomach bulging from the meal, the cat soon became wedged in the fork of a tree. Two monkeys helped free it, but the ungrateful leopard then ate one of them. The other hurled abuse from high on a branch and cursed the cat to walk alone for all eternity.

We wait several minutes after the leopard leaves before approaching the lake, which is shaped like an eggplant and several acres in size. After inspecting the shore and finding no dinosaur tracks, I wade into the purplish water, which never comes above my waist. We collect a few giant mollusks and a dozen lake snails with handsome shells as big as croquet balls. Unwittingly, I also collect a few leeches, and Innocent helps burn them off with a lit cigarette.

On our way back to the pirogue, Innocent stops next to a baobab tree, perhaps the most useful tree in the tropics. The pulp of its fruit is used as a seasoning; the young leaves are eaten as a vegetable; the seeds are pounded into meal; the ashes from the bark are a good soap; and, Innocent says, stripping away sections of the inner bark, "It's great for making rope and cloth." In a couple of minutes he plaits lengths of the inner bark into a serviceable net to hold our catch of snails and mollusks.

Heaving the net over his shoulder, he says he feels like a Fang storyteller, men who go from village to village along the Atlantic coast carrying nets filled with items both common and rare. "I met one guy with dried-up fingers, teeth, hooves, stones, ship models, paint cans . . . locks of hair, beads, old socks . . . even a refrigerator handle," Innocent tells me. For a fee, they tell fantastic stories about any item in their net. "If you picked the same thing twice, he had two different stories to tell."

At the other end of the lake, we see a welcoming plume of white smoke, suggesting that the others have had a successful hunt.

"Escargots!" We hold out the giant snails as we enter the camp.

"Monkey! Snake! Lizard" Theo replies, pointing to the carcasses they're butchering. Gabriel and Raymond stand erect and hold up something stretched between them. It's an impressive twelve-foot-long python, as thick as my arm and missing its head. Raymond boasts that his spear hit the snake and "took the head off in one throw."

At dinnertime, Innocent and I pass up the monkey stew for a surf-and-turf combination of snail and reptile. The python is greasy and chewy, but not unpleasant tasting; the snail is less appealing, its flavor reminding me of a vitamin pill. As usual, we all eat with our fingers; at this point, forks and napkins seem like distant memories. I mention that a scotch on the rocks would perk up the meal, but the men from Boha don't understand. They've never seen an ice cube, and snow is something that happens on television screens in Epena; my attempts to describe ice only puzzle them further.

Ange asks Innocent for details about the satellite lake we explored, and as he reports its location and shape, Ange starts cursing us.

"Idiots! That is sacred land. Taboo . . ."

"Was that where you saw Mokele-Mbembe?" Gabriel blurts, then tightens his lips, sorry he opened his mouth.

Ange stares at his friend, and Gabriel looks away. I sit up, waiting for a reply. Ange, like everyone from Boha, doesn't like talking about Mokele-Mbembe. When he does, it's almost always a story someone long dead has told him.

"I don't know what I saw . . . It was big."

"Big as Mokele-Mbembe?" I ask.

He turns his back to me, and when I repeat my question, he shakes his fist, spits on the ground, and threatens me with Raymond's spear.

"Bonne nuit." Gabriel ushers me, Innocent, and Theo into the tent and suggests that we turn in early. The three of us poke our heads through the tent opening and see Gabriel apologizing to Ange. In a few minutes they shake hands, and Gabriel curls up next to the fire. Ange walks toward the lake, where he stands and stares out over the water.

"Maybe he saw a dinosaur or maybe he saw something much bigger," Innocent speculates.

That night I dream of sauropods as big as the Empire State Building.

CHAPTER ◆ 26

A DEEP SOUND RUMBLES through the jungle as we're eating dinner later in the week. It's the Boha village drum pounding out a message: someone in Djéké has just died. Raymond groans.

"A friend of yours?" I ask.

"Worse . . . an enemy."

Raymond excuses himself and walks off talking aloud. We soon hear the whacking of his machete, and he returns to the fire carrying a bundle of saplings, which he strips of leaves and fashions into an arch. We help him install it in front of a lean-to and watch as he selects some items from his juju bag to suspend from the top of the arch.

"Protection," Innocent says quietly. He explains that revenge is a far greater threat from the dead than from the living, and the most dangerous period is the interlude between death and burial. Normally the spirit moves on once the corpse is in the ground but until then, it can go on a rampage. The pygmy rail we heard days ago may have been someone's spirit in such a state. The fetish-strewn archway will protect Raymond while he sleeps tonight, unguarded by his shadow spirit.

"I didn't know the man," Raymond tells us, tucking a small doll under his pillow of leaves, but his family and the dead man's family have been locked in a blood feud for two generations. "My father met the man once, I think. It all happened in my grandfather's time." If the man's death was caused by a visible wound, things won't get worse between the families. However, if he died of internal causes, Raymond believes that he and his family will be accused of murder.

"They will say we put a curse on him," he observes.

"Did you?" Theo asks.

"Of course we did. Our families are enemies."

The state won't get involved in the dispute, but the witch doctors in Djéké and Boha surely will, casting spells and counterspells for their clients. "My family must be protected from that man's evil," Raymond says, confident that his father is with the witch doctor right now, engineering the family's defense. Before we go to sleep, Theo hangs a charm from his juju bag above the tent flap. "Extra insurance," he says, kissing the charm.

Getting dressed has become the most distasteful part of my morning, and I bitch and moan while slithering into my clammy rags. My old shoes have now deteriorated into sandals of a sort, held together by duct tape and vanilla-bean vine. It has been ten days since we left Boha, and all of us have grown beards except Gabriel, who likes to stroke the few hairs that sprout on his chin while urging them to grow and multiply.

Since the soaking that greeted our arrival at the lake, we have had good weather, that is, partly sunny days followed by a sunset shower and a midnight downpour. We've all established routines — for example, my day always begins with some birding before dawn. So far I've identified seventy-eight species around Télé, including a pygmy woodpecker, only three inches long and a rare, unexpected sight; most likely a jungle storm blew it here from its usual haunts in Cameroon. The hunters have had excellent luck, and the food locker is almost filled to capacity with salted meats. Innocent and I, though, haven't found a single trace of Mokele-Mbembe. In fact, we haven't seen a four-legged creature of any sort in almost a week, not since spotting the leopard at what Innocent now calls Taboo Lake. All the molombo vines we monitor are intact, not one fruit missing, and the goliath heron is the largest animal I've sighted on Lake Télé. We've investigated all but one of the inlets and most of the jungle within a mile of the lake, and our most extraordinary discovery has been a leech the size of a vacuum cleaner nozzle.

For the first few days at the lake, I tried luring butterflies with snake and lizard meat, as one American lepidopterist had suggested. A few swallowtails came, but no blues, whites, julias, or nymphalids. Then one day I left a pair of ripe socks at the end of a stick to dry, and butterflies by the dozens fluttered to them, obviously attracted by my irresistible odor. Every morning since, I've been using the same technique. Today's visitors include the rare *Salamis cacta cacta*, a handsome chestnut-brown butterfly with a blush of violet on its forewings.

Innocent intends to spend the day fishing once again for the giant perch, so I head out alone in the other pirogue for Bompale Stream, the last inlet left to explore. Again water lilies clog the mouth of the inlet, and it takes me almost two hours to cut a path through them. I pole to the jungle side of the tunnel and moor the pirogue, sighting a water chevrotain while tying up the boat. This squat, deerlike animal with spotted tan fur, staggers left, then right, before turning left again and dashing off. I walk beside the shallow Bompale for several kilometers until a snapping of twigs brings me to a stop under an ironwood tree. The noise comes and goes, but my attention is diverted by a giant millipede, eight inches long and rust red in color, racing past my foot. Though harmless, millipedes are considered evil in Congolese folklore; when I tried to catch one earlier, Innocent held me back, saying I would get leprosy and possibly infect him. This particular one, the largest I've ever seen, nearly fills a bug-collecting jar. It has 112 pairs of legs, by my quick count.

The crackling of twigs erupts into a loud crashing. There's a swath of freshly trampled ferns and arum plants up ahead, and I cautiously start to follow it.

"Bah-grumph," something says. I climb a tree buttress to scan the area. Nothing unusual.

"Mokele-Mbembe?"

"Bah-grumph . . . gumpa-pa."

A tremendous noise rends the air. A liana tumbles to the ground, whacking limbs and leaves as it falls through the middle canopy. Seconds later some heavy-footed creature starts barreling through the brush. I break into a trot to catch up with it. Eventually, saplings start bending just ahead of me, and I glimpse a dark form just as a foul odor hits me. The creature veers right and enters a clearing. It's black and hairy and hunched, with a white, almost silvery band running above its rump. I've been trailing a western lowland gorilla, a large silverback male.

I pull up short, acutely aware that the massive knuckle-walker can bend me into a pretzel. Thankfully, the gorilla continues on its noisy way, grumbling, grunting, and snorting. Listening to its unearthly sounds, half-animal and half-human, I wonder how often a gorilla has been mistaken for Mokele-Mbembe.

All around me are fallen trees in various stages of decomposition, a perfect breeding ground for beetles. I'm still hunting for one to name after my fourth-grade teacher; to qualify, it must be particularly ugly, with a countenance inspiring fear, and it must be a new species, of course. I don't find an appropriate specimen, but I do manage to capture an attractive green and black beetle, as well as a dozen others in different shades of purple.

▼

Come four o'clock in the afternoon, cocktail hour, as I'm packing up the insects and tweezers, I suddenly realize that I'm lost. While chasing the gorilla, I failed to mark my trail. I sense that the pirogue lies somewhere to the southeast, so I trudge off in that direction, this time notching trees with my machete and constantly referring to my compass. The light is fading fast, the guenons are grunting, and a hornbill blares out like a ship's horn in the fog. As evening falls, the thin cries of bats echo overhead, and night-walking galagos start their day, greeting neighbors with high-pitched yips and yaps. A West African wood owl calls its ghostly "whoo-whoot-who-who." Like the pygmy rails, owls are believed to be agents of evil spirits. I close my mouth and cover my ears.

Without the sun's warmth, the moist air in the canopy quickly condenses. Droplets ploink down on me, the ground temperature starts to drop, and I begin to feel cold, but instead of making a fire and hunkering down for the night, I press on, expecting to stumble on Bompale Stream and the pirogue. All around me creatures bark, groan, whir and purr, peep, churr, whoop and croak. Mosquitoes hum and fireflies blink amorously, while their terrestrial cousins, *Gephitomorpha* centipedes, glow like bits of neon crawling along the ground. Small animals occasionally dart across my path; sometimes they pause to stare at me, but most seem neither frightened nor particularly interested. Whenever I flick on the flashlight, moths fly toward it, knocking into my head, shoulders, and hands. Spider webs, a nuisance during the day, turn into messy tussles when I run into them at night.

My watch reads 11:55 when I hear the splashing of water under my feet. It's neither Bompale Stream nor Lake Télé, but I'm too tired to care and too thirsty to be particular. After straining some water through my handkerchief and taking a drink, I decide to build a fire, resigned to spending the night alone.

To make kindling I use the machete like a draw plane and skim off shavings from a fallen tree. A few pages from a field guide serve as the wick. The paper ignites readily, but the wood hardly sweats. I try again, crumpling more pages, and toss on a roll of film, which emits a kaleidoscope of colors, yet the wood merely smokes. Some gauze bandaging plus the indexes from my field guides and the alcohol from my bug jars finally jolt a fire to life. I pile on some branches, hoping the flames will deter visits from inquisitive cats. After a spare meal of one Camel, with another Camel for dessert, I lie down for the night.

I quickly slip into a deep sleep, and Morpheus carries my soul to the edge of a sea. Waves are breaking with deafening thuds; the night sky is streaked with crimson clouds lined in gold. A sauropod rises from the ocean depths, sucking in air like a giant turbine. Water sheets down its massive flanks. The beast thunders up the beach, shaking the earth. Slowly it lowers its head, its giant, vulgar eyes glaring at me, and its mouth opens, revealing a lone tooth. I begin walking into its maw.

Startled awake by something cold and wet rubbing my cheek, I find a lungfish wiggling next to me. I flick it into the water with my machete. The fire is still blazing as I return to sleep, this time dead to any world.

An early morning cloudburst rousts me as well as my uninvited bedmates, some two dozen cockroaches and several carabid beetles. The beetles look benign, but this species is able to eject a caustic fluid that blisters the skin. Luckily, none of them seems to regard me as anything but a heat source. Ever since Theo found a scorpion in his boot, I've whacked my shoes before putting them on; today a caterpillar falls out. I survey the area in the faint blue light of dawn and find before me again the forbidden Taboo Lake, where Ange maybe saw Mokele-Mbembe. A pair of bronze-naped pigeons drink at its edge; mistletoe berries are stuck to their beaks and necks.

After a hearty breakfast Camel, I move out, now certain where the pirogue lies. When I'm halfway there, a black-throated honey guide jabbers at me, "Kerr-kerr . . .," and darts to the west. It returns and impatiently repeats the call. These birds are among the very few undomesticated animals that naturally seek out humans as partners. Honey guides feed on beeswax and lead humans to the usually well-hidden hives. The men smoke out the bees and collect the honey, leaving bits of the comb for the bird. Of all the symbiotic relationships in the rain forest, this is the only one I've witnessed that includes man. At another time I might follow it, but not today. I'm anxious to return to camp before the others are up.

Leaves rustle, and a piece of wood snaps to my left. "Kerr kerr," the honey guide rants, and three Pygmies step from behind a tree. I hear a sound behind me and turn to see two more emerge from behind another tree. Naked except for belts of liana, with short hair and no discernible tribal markings or jewelry, they stand only four and a half feet tall. Their skin is lighter than the Bantus', more red than black, and though their legs are short, the Pygmies have long torsos and large feet. Their hands, too, seem disproportionately big, with thick, powerful fingers.

I smile. They don't.

Two of them carry crossbows and quivers crammed with arrows. The other three tote iron-tipped spears and feathered blowguns. All of them have machetes as well. They walk toward me, one man, presumably their leader, a step ahead. His restless eyes seem to be examining every square inch of me. He says something, and they all stop. The headman slowly opens his mouth, exposing a few rotten teeth, and utters a shrill sound.

"Bonjour!" I reply.

He stares at me in silence. I turn and step to one side, trying to keep all the Pygmies in view at once.

The leader ululates again, this time holding a high note for several seconds. I stand motionless until he stops, then venture a greeting in Lingala. The headman slouches and picks at his navel. The two Pygmies on my right join their companions, and they all start talking among themselves. I can't understand anything they're saying. They stop their conversation and take a few steps toward me, sniffing the air as they walk. From the way they rub their noses, it seems they don't like my odor. That, at least, is understandable.

"Following the honey guide?" I try in English, flapping my arms. Now they seem amused. The headman nods as I continue fanning the air. "Kerr-kerr," I add, pointing up at the honey guide.

"Kerrar . . ." one man sings, rendering a perfect imitation of the bird. He has puffy cheeks and a cleft in his round chin. Like the others, he has silky skin and no facial hair; he could be fourteen or forty.

"Tokay," I say and point to the honey guide.

"Kerrar," the man instructs.

The headman shouts something that sounds like "Surf's Up."

"Tokay."

He repeats himself, and I suggest that we follow the honey guide together, acting out my words as if we're playing charades. The Pygmies stand silent. I take a step toward the bird, and they all shout at me. I smile and shrug my shoulders. They stare at me quizzically. I hold out my hand. The headman takes a swipe at it with his crossbow. We're not making a good connection.

"Listen." I pull out my harmonica. The Hohner Marine

Band seems to delight them. "Take it," I offer, handing the harmonica to the bird caller. He passes it around and they all smile. But then, as I dip into my shoulder bag again and pull out a camera, the headman becomes alarmed. Perhaps, like certain desert tribesmen, he believes cameras are evil instruments that capture the soul. He shrieks louder than ever and doesn't let up even when I put the camera away. The man next to me loads and cocks his crossbow. I don't know what's wrong, but I better do something to calm everyone. I notice that the headman has an infected cut on his right foot that's oozing yellow-green pus. I drop to my knees and pull out my medical kit; everyone stares as I walk on my knees toward the headman.

"Aarrgh!" the man shouts, kicking me in the throat the moment my hand touches his wound. The cotton and antiseptic fly through the air. The Pygmies howl and whoop, and one of them starts pumping his spear, aiming at my head. I raise my hands and slowly rise from my knees. The man drops the spear tip to the ground, and the others huddle and begin talking quietly. The headman gestures at the honey guide and then flicks his hand at me.

"Kerrar," the singer trills, and his companions nod.

The man with the harmonica plays a sour note, but his friend with the cocked crossbow grabs his wrist and motions toward the bird. The harmonica disappears inside a quiver. The headman declares something and, curiously, all the Pygmies show their backs and start walking away. After they've gone three steps toward the honey guide, I bolt the other way, weaving through the underbrush, and run as fast as I can all the way to the pirogue.

Back at camp, Ange berates me for staying out all night. "Where did you sleep, white fool?" he scolds.

"Near the shore, close to Bompale Stream," I lie, not wanting him to know I was anywhere near Taboo Lake.

When the others go hunting, Innocent confides that Ange was more worried than mad. "But Ange would never admit that, so he yelled at you instead."

I tell him about the gorilla, the night in the jungle, and the Pygmies.

"You touched his foot! Mon Dieu," Innocent exclaims, throwing his hands over his head. "What were you thinking?"

"I was just trying to help."

"You almost got yourself killed. Forest Pygmies don't know about medicine. He probably believes you caused the wound . . . No one would touch a wound unless they had put the curse on and were trying to make it worse."

The fact that I'm still alive proves one of two things to Innocent: either I'm blessed with luck or I'm being watched over by the wind god, as the witch doctor predicted. At the moment, he doesn't care which it is as long as I'm still alive. "If you die, I'll be swamped in paperwork. Do you realize the number of reports and forms I would have to fill out? It would be hell for me."

"It would be hell for both of us," I interject, and promise to be more careful.

CHAPTER ◆ 27

TODAY WE CATCH grandfather lizards," Raymond announces, standing in the bow of the pirogue, one hand shielding his eyes and the other under his nose. "That way!" He points to the northeastern shore. "I can smell them."

Yet again the wind gods have nothing to say to us mortals. Gumball-shaped clouds linger in the sky, waiting for a breeze. Smooth as porcelain, Lake Télé steams in the morning sunshine. The humidity is 100 percent and the temperature, as usual, is 90 degrees in the shade.

Two large cormorants, each a meter long, dry their wings on a partially submerged log. The color of wet licorice, with long flexible necks, they slip into the water as we approach. One of them never surfaces, at least not within view, and its mate moves away with only its neck and head above water, forming the first question mark of the day.

Signaling for me to steer to starboard, Raymond cocks his arm and launches a spear, cursing when it hits a cycad. Something jumps through the bush.

"Golden cat," Innocent says. "It was beautiful. You should have seen it."

"Shh," Raymond hushes, his eyes skyward.

A crowned hawk eagle tucks its broad wings and dives. A few dozen feet from the treetops, the raptor unfurls its wings, corrects the angle of attack, and flashes its talons. Monkeys howl, but the hawk eagle snatches one aloft. It flails for several seconds before going limp, looking distressingly like a child as the bird carries it east and out of sight.

We cut across the lake, leaving plenty of room between ourselves and the birds congregating on the northern shore. A flock of egrets pose like figures on a Japanese screen, while ducks waddle clumsily along the shore. As we near the western beach, Raymond orders us to reverse course and head back the way we came.

"It doesn't smell right over here."

We cruise the opposite shore for an hour, sighting nothing unusual, when suddenly Raymond's eyes open wide. He ships his spear and leans outboard. A turtle is just below the surface about fifteen yards away. "Bare hands," Raymond promises. As we come alongside, he bends over the rail and deftly scoops it into the bilge. The turtle pulls in its yellow-streaked head and retracts its flippers and tail, but Raymond nonchalantly plunges a knife into the head opening, working the blade like a reamer.

"I love turtle meat, don't you?" Raymond asks as blood and guts spill into the bilge. Innocent and I remain silent.

We keep going, still looking for a grandfather lizard, finally giving up late in the afternoon to head back in for, yes, turtle soup.

Waiting for me next to the tent, under a T-shirt that has

fallen off a drying rack, is the ugliest beetle I've ever seen. It's the size of a cough lozenge and the color of phlegm, rimmed in black. I carefully pack it in a special jar, and unable to find anything like it in the field guide, I print on the label "Sister Marie Bernadette."

Early the next morning I find a molombo vine with several

fruits missing. There are no dinosaur footprints about, and I hurry on to check the two other molombos. Fruit is missing from the second vine as well. However, also in view is a blue plantain-eater, lustily devouring the fruit of the god-beast. As it noshes, the black crop atop the bird's head flops from side to side.

Back at camp, Innocent tells me that he dreamed about Mokele-Mbembe. "He spoke to me . . . Today is the day he appears . . . I've made two offerings already this morning."

That's fine, I say, but I'm beginning to doubt that any dinosaur has passed this way in the last sixty-five million years. I suggest we break camp tomorrow and head west-northwest, along the edge of Pygmy territory. Ange checks the food locker and returns nodding his head; we have plenty of meat, and everyone but Innocent is ready to leave the lake. Theo, however, groans at the mention of a westward march. He wants to go back to Boha.

"A week heading west means another week walking home," Ange says. "That's too long." Theo beams at his hunting partner.

We strike a compromise: tomorrow we'll head into the uncharted jungle, angling for the headwaters of the Bai River. We figure its a two-day walk there and another three days back to Boha.

Gabriel and Raymond decide to join Innocent and me for the last day of what Gabriel calls "boating." Innocent and I sit amidships, listening to Captain Raymond bicker with Captain Gabriel while we cruise the shoreline for game. As we slip into the shadow of a meni oil tree, several leaves flutter into the bilge, and soon the air is filled with leaves. Within minutes, this 150-foot giant loses half its foliage. Leaf fall in the jungle is an irregular happening and depends on the tree's internal rhythm, but Raymond insists that the gods have undressed the tree spirit for us.

"We've been blessed. Some powerful god must be very close," Gabriel agrees, rubbing his hand across his juju bag. Tree spirits, he reasons, want to keep their leaves, letting go of them only when commanded by a greater spirit.

A herd of jungle elephants trumpet in the distance; Raymond and Gabriel reflexively ready their weapons, only to sit down and relax seconds later.

"Too much trouble . . . Let the Pygmies eat them," Gabriel sighs, and explains that the Pygmies inject poison into bananas, which they scatter in bunches for the elephants; when one dies from the toxin, they simply set up camp around the carcass. The only elephant Gabriel ever killed wasn't worth the effort. "I shot it twice, but it kept walking and walking . . . Two days until it finally dropped to the ground." The meat grew rancid by the time he lugged it back to Boha.

"Ho-chor!" Gabriel wags a finger to starboard.

All I can see is flat, calm water. "Crocodile?" I ask.

"No . . . See it? Over there. Look, over there."

There's something moving in the water near the far shore, probably a large bird of some type.

"I see! . . . Yeee!" Gabriel's voice rises to a crescendo. He starts paddling for the closest land.

"Ho-chor! I see him now," Raymond begins poling double-time and speaking hurriedly with Gabriel in Lingala. The only word I catch is Mokele-Mbembe.

I snatch up my binoculars and grab the camera and telephoto lens from my bag. Raymond lays into his push pole, dripping sweat. Gabriel casts furtive glances about and starts yelling, "Faster . . . faster."

Thud. The pirogue rams the shore and Gabriel leaps out.

Raymond cuffs me on the shoulder and orders me out of the boat. In my viewfinder, I've almost got something in focus, a dark, slender form.

"Mundélé, move!"

A hand clamps onto my shoulder blade. I look up and see Raymond with his fist clenched.

I climb ashore and lift my camera again; now I can see clearly a black periscope shape in the water, about a kilometer away.

"Mokele-Mbembe?" I ask.

"Oui, Mokele-Mbembe . . . Mokele-Mbembe," Raymond and Gabriel shout, bowing their heads as they speak the name.

Innocent sights through the binoculars as I click off some pictures, unsatisfied with what I see through the lens: the elongated black form that curves in on itself is only a vague image. It might have a spoon-shaped head, but I can't tell for sure. Indeed, from this distance, it's impossible to judge its size or accurately discern its features. I ask Gabriel and Raymond to paddle me closer to the animal in the lake.

"No. We stay here and pray." Raymond falls to his knees, and Gabriel joins him.

"I'll pay you."

Raymond angrily slaps the ground and tells me to kneel.

"Ten thousand francs."

No one responds.

"Fifteen thousand."

Still no response. Both men have grabbed their juju bags and shut their eyes. The creature is moving on a steady course that won't bring it close to us. I throw down my wallet. "It's all yours if we go." Raymond and Gabriel mutter in Lingala.

"They're cursing you," Innocent warns. "You go. I'll take care of them."

I sprint for the pirogue, shove off, and jump aboard. I dig in the paddle, and the boat surges forward, faster and faster, as if I've entered a magnetic field drawing me to its center. I hear angry voices behind me, calling my name, and there's a lot of splashing in the water, but I keep my eyes straight ahead. Though still a silhouette, the black form is a bit clearer now, looking like a splendid French curve, thick at the base and tapering to a hooked tip, where it flattens and gets thick again. I keep paddling, hoping to identify a face presumed lost in fossilized rocks millions of years ago.

"Arrêtez! . . . Arrêtez!" Innocent shrieks.

I turn and see Raymond and Gabriel running in the shallows. Raymond has his spear at the ready, his forearm tensed behind his head; Gabriel has the shotgun trained on me. I drop the paddle.

"Retournez! Retournez!" Innocent pleads, standing at the water's edge and waving me in.

Turning my back to the creature of the lake, I pick up the paddle and head to shore. When my feet touch land, Gabriel clicks on the safety and pulls a shell from the chamber of the shotgun.

Innocent helps me beach the pirogue, his hands shaking. Gabriel and Raymond return to their prayers. The form continues southward until it suddenly disappears, submerging a half-mile away. Innocent and I study the lake, but all remains calm; nothing breaks the water's mirrored surface. In all, the creature stayed in view for seven minutes and thirty-two seconds, moving through water seven to eight feet deep. I estimate its speed at two knots; Innocent thinks it was moving twice as fast.

"Fool," Raymond shouts, rising from his knees and storming my way. "The god can approach man, but man NEVER approaches the god. He would have killed us all." He spins toward Gabriel, and they whisper to each other. Gabriel slaps his friend on the shoulder and either laughs or snorts, I can't tell which.

We paddle back to camp without further incident, and Innocent and I sit by the lake watching a shoal of butterflies devour my last sock. I take out my notebook and write down the day's observations, starting on a new page under the headline GOD-

BEAST SURFACES. My selective account seems to gain credibility with each sentence and soon acquires a remarkable similarity to unvarnished fact.

Innocent points down the western trail; Ange and Theo are returning from their day of hunting. Theo carries a green monkey by its tail. The men from Boha talk, and we tell Theo about the sighting. Ange is surprisingly calm. If anyone suffers, he says almost sweetly, it will be me; if Mokele-Mbembe has been angered, I will pay the price.

"If you awake in the morning, we leave Télé as planned; if you die, we bury you here. Agreed?"

"Agreed."

We start cleaning up the camp and collecting our equipment. Theo stands next to me, watching each piece of gear go into a bag and asking if he can have it when I die.

◆

"Hey, are you alive?" Innocent shakes me awake. "It's dawn, well, almost dawn."

Today is the first morning that we're all up at the same early hour. We drink coffee spiked with the last of the scotch, and Innocent and Theo talk about the creature of the lake. Remarkably, Theo's description is the liveliest.

In the fuzzy tradition of Loch Ness sightings, Mokele-Mbembe has left us to argue the fine details about its black form. The water hid its body and swallowed any tracks. Maybe, as Innocent suggests, it was just a vulcanodon, a midget-sized brontosaurus, standing about seven feet at the shoulder, with the signature long neck of a sauropod. Even the experts who review my photographs later in New York aren't sure what has been captured, and none of them will go on record one way or the other.

"You got what you came for, eh, my friend?" Gabriel asks me.

"Sure he did," Theo interjects. "The dinosaur was bigger than any of us imagined. I mean it was *huge . . .*"

Gabriel winks at Raymond, who smiles and nudges Ange, who nods at me as he counts the money I've just handed him for use of the pirogues, one of many fees not mentioned in Boha. "Bring rich friends next time," Gabriel says.

"Tokay," Ange shouts, pocketing the cash and pouring water on the campfire. A great cloud of steam rises into the middle canopy.

We shoulder our bags packed with gear and salted meat, flies and bees buzzing around us. We each pluck a leaf from a sapling and stow it safely in a pocket. Once we reach Boha, we'll breathe into the leaves and give thanks as we place them at the base of another sapling. Falling in line behind Ange, we set off down the western trail, aiming for the upper Bai and Sangha rivers, where others have reported sightings of twenty-ton dinosaurs.

It's not long, though, before Ange drops his pack and detours back to the lake. The six of us walk out on a fallen tree jutting over the water. On our left the lake surface reflects our images, and off to the right our shadows float in the water. Ange recites a short prayer of thanksgiving to Mokele-Mbembe and then faces his shadow. We follow his example.

"Say good-bye," Innocent advises. "I doubt we'll see our shadow spirits again for days."

When we return to the trail, the men from Boha hunch over a pool of mud and use their forefingers to draw three concentric circles. They quickly move on, but I linger, staring at their design as it dissolves in the watery mud. Perhaps, as Bantu myth recommends, the line of life is an ever-tightening circle, a python that greedily grabs its tail at birth and keeps on swallowing, never realizing what's nourishing it until it's too late.

"Hurry up," Ange calls. "We have a long way to go."

EPILOGUE ◆

A CROSS THE AISLE of the plane, a woman brushes her hands across her lap as if she's whisking off cigarette ash. I stare at her, which only makes her hands move faster.

"She thinks someone has cursed her, so she's trying to sweep the curse your way. The evil spirit has to go somewhere," Innocent says, glad he took the window seat.

The witch doctor in Boha reclaimed the protective spirits he had loaned me, and according to Innocent, my bumble in the jungle has exhausted the power of my juju bag.

"Madame, s'il vous plaît, autre part. Okay?"

"Pardon, monsieur," she says, redirecting the curse toward the man sitting in front of me.

The commandant and Theo wave to us as the Air Congo plane sputters to life, its left engine misfiring and belching smoke before settling into a steady thunder. The postmaster sits on his moped in the middle of the crowd and salutes while the plane taxis to the end of the airstrip. He's wearing his jacket, pants, and official blue cap, but no shirt. Off to one side by themselves are the six paddlers from Boha who brought us to Epena in record time, eleven hours and twenty-six minutes, enabling us to catch this flight to Brazzaville. They're drinking whiskey and wearing new clothes bought, no doubt, with the money they charged for the trip. Most everyone in Epena has turned out to watch the plane lift off; it's the last flight before the airport officially closes for the rainy season.

"There they are!" Innocent points out the window at three men on the terminal roof. It's Marc, Gaspar, and Alain. Drumsticks in hand, they're pounding the metal roof panels.

◆

Back in Brazzaville, Robert, glad to have his poker partner back, moves someone out of my old room and hands me the familiar key to number seven. He's delighted with the crossbow I present him and hangs it on the wall in the lobby. Before leaving, I catch him stalking a pied crow with it in the hotel garden. My collection of flora and fauna goes to the university. The administrator handling my donation assures me each item will be studied, identified, and catalogued, and hands me a receipt saying, "Accepted with thanks, three plastic garbage bags."

AFTERWORD   ◆

SEGMENTED WORMS the size of school buses, which breed
off the California coast, grab my attention. The world's
largest earwigs were last sighted on Saint Helena Island in
1967, and I wonder what happened to them. Unconfirmed
reports of killer snails with painted shells as big as Volkswagen
bugs sound intriguing, certainly worth checking out. Where is
that darn Tasmanian tiger anyway? Meandering in the jet
stream also has its appeal, as does stumbling on a rare desert
bloom. What exactly colors those white blanks on a world
map? I'd like to know. Since none of my friends will join me
on these investigations of the obscure, I'll probably take off
alone.

However, without friends, I'd be homebound. Heather
Schroder, David Rottner, and Ike Williams fend off ill-man-
nered collection agencies. Virginia Reath and Kevin Cahill

prepare my medical kits and debug me after I return; Virginia's salves are wondrous. James Angell, my writing partner, and Harry Foster and Peg Anderson keep the words flowing; George Trow maintains the level of what's interesting. Thinking back to Brazzaville, I remember fondly the help of the Lukenses, Tuckers, Sieferts, and Laxenaires. Family, of course, is important, especially my brother, Conn. Bing West pulls strings I dare not touch. Virginia Creeper develops the images and sets the tone, while Elizabeth McFadden, my love, reads, edits, advises, and somehow deals with it all.